After studying at St Martins School of Art and following a career in fashion, Ms Kais dedicated her time to painting.

In 2011, she was inspired to write her first book, a biography, 'London is the Place for Me'.

Bel Kais lives in London.

To Bobbie x Diana,
with love,
Bel Hair.

London is the Place for Me

Best Wishes
all the Best
from
Sterling
Mr BE

London is the Place for Me

Bel Kais

ARTEMIS PUBLISHERS

ISBN-978-1-907785-13 9

First Published in 2013
ARTEMIS PUBLISHERS LTD.

Hamilton House
Mabledon Place
Bloomsbury
London
WC1H 9BB

www.artemispublishers.com

Printed & Bound in Great Britain

Dedication

Benjamin and Katherine

Acknowledgements

Sarah Ford of Artemis for having believed in this book.
Benjamin Betancourt for his magnanimous support.
Brian Cecil Awang for his altruism.

"RIEN DE GRAND NE S'EST ACCOMPLI DANS LE MONDE SANS PASSION"

Georg Wilhelm Fredrich Hegel

Chapter I
"In Trinidad there was a family..."

Sitting on the edge of the sofa playing the Cuatro, Sterling, with expressive impersonation is singing, 'Shame and Scandal in the Family", a song written in 1943 by Sir Lancelot, the Calypsonian and Trinidadian, as he had pointed out to me earlier on. When the words of the song escape him, he hums the melody and by placing the Cuatro on his knees, uses it like a drum and taps it in rhythm for accompaniment. Like all great performers Sterling, through his passion for music, communicates with a natural aptitude it seems, an incredible 'joie de vivre'.

I met Sterling Betancourt many years ago after a performance he had given in a London hall. It was my first introduction to Steel Band and, like many others, was persuaded by Sterling's enthusiastic attitude that I also could play and learn many tunes, only to later discover that his convincing way of making you believe that everyone has the talent and ability to master this instrument, eventually brings you to the harsh reality of not possessing the most essential ingredients required to master this art: timing, dexterity and rhythm.

At rehearsals, I have seen Sterling's unlimited patience and perseverance at getting out of you the little predisposition, or the little talent, you may have for being a good pan player and will, out of sheer enjoyment for this instrument, build you up and make you believe in your own genius!

Sterling stopped singing and it brought me back to the present as I was transported years ago when, after having had dinner at his house, I was to observe the many pictures and awards decorating the lavatory walls and when I remarked what an unusual place it was to have all these rather amazing marks of recognition for his pioneering steel band, laughingly he had answered, "I think that on the contrary, it is very appropriate, you see, I enjoy very much having a salute of some sort, in the meantime I need to knock off my ego a bit, so this is the best place!"

Despite all the years Sterling has lived in England he has retained his Trinidadian accent, even if he argues that he could never live in Trinidad again, he has for the past ten years been a frequent visitor to the island, spending many months at a time with his close friend, Brian Awang, in Diego Martin.

Not many poets or voyagers have celebrated the beauty of Trinidad, while Tobago, its twin sister, has so far gathered all the attention in the description of its sandy beaches, turquoise sea and paradise island. Trinidad, in spite of the many beauties and interests it shelters, is mostly known for its carnival and steel band and unfortunately building itself a reputation for not being now a safe place to be.

Times have changed, new generation, new import and influences, quite distant is the time of sleeping with doors and windows open.

For centuries the island had remained a closed world and despite the removal of man's freedom, life had pursued the course of tradition where man had retained his intimate contact with the soil and its roots.

When reading this, Sterling cannot prevent a comment with a sarcastic laugh, "Have they really? When was the last time you were in Trinidad?"

Laventille

Sterling was born in Laventille, a suburb on the eastern fringe of the capital, Port of Spain, east of the St Anne river, known as 'the dry river' (so called as so little water flows into it out of the rainy season), it stretches from the lowlands, along the eastern main road into the hills above the capital, divided into the 'up the hill' area and the 'down the hill'.

This working class area was known for being the home of the deprived and the immigrants from the nearby islands, attracted by the many jobs at the wharfs of Port of Spain. The most violent neighbourhood but also the principal birth place of the Steel Pan.

In 1930, when Sterling was born, the last of four children, the houses clinging to the hills were mostly shacks built on stilts, most with one window and one door. Sterling's mother, Stella Bowen, nicknamed 'Mywo', worked as a seamstress, a cook and a cleaner, her husband, Edwin

Betancourt, like his seven brothers, was a musician, he played the banjo and the guitar and to make ends meet was a jack of all trades and worked as a shoemaker, a barber, a mason and at many other jobs.

Having left his Cuatro on the sofa, I follow Sterling into the kitchen and just look at his way of preparing tea in silence, not too bothered that the red kettle is whistling and steaming the window, he seems distracted and lost in thoughts. Only when he joins me at the table does he reconnect again with our previous conversation and then, having recollected his thoughts, and without any invite on my part, immerses himself in narrating his childhood memories.

"If my father never cared for his children, he was a very good musician, not that I knew much of him, as he left home when I was two, but I often heard people referring to him as a talented banjo player, who was asked by many bands. My older brother Herman has a better recollection of him and of his neglectful and dismissing attitude towards us. I must say that my parents were very young when they had their children, my mother was only fifteen when pregnant with her first child, she was immediately kicked out of her great grandparent's house where she lived at the time and was taken in by the neighbours who looked after her. Her mother, Maude, was already living in Venezuela and had married there. Stella and her sister Doris were the daughters of a married man, Sam Bowen, a merchant, who Maude had an affair with in Laventille. Sam had thirty children, scattered all over the islands and all from different women... At an early age, my sister Sheila and brother Herman went to live with my great grand, while I remained with my mum, (I never knew my other brother who died at three, before I was born). Only much later did I realise how hard it must have been for my mother to raise all of us alone while she worked in the quarry breaking stones, often taking me with her and, as a 4 year-old helped her piling the pebbles in a heap for the trucks to carry them to building sites.

Our house was not very far from the quarry and when they dynamited the quarry, bits of stones fell on our roof. As a warning and before the blast, a man would walk through the streets ringing a bell and carrying a red flag to notify people to stay away as an explosion in the quarry was about to take place.

We lived in Ovid Alley, a dirt track, off Laventille Road. The alley was lined with mango, coconut trees and other varieties which, as children, we often tried to climb and I, after having had a bad fall, kept well away from making any further attempt. Separated by all this vegetation, the wooden houses had enough space underneath for the coal pot where my mother cooked and where I played. Fires often broke out this way, setting the whole house on fire. Our house consisted of one room, It was a multipurpose room with a bed that I did not share with my mother as I often wetted the bed, so I slept on the floor. There were ducks and chickens in the back yard and under the house, where, once, when I saw a rat catching a duckling and carrying it away, I was so terrified that I never played there again. There were no street lights in Ovid Alley nor running water and in order to wash I had to walk to the stand pipe in Laventille Road, where other children gathered and played, never forgetting to bring a bucket of water home. Only the main roads were then installed with electric lights.

At the age of four, Mywo sent me to kindergarten in Quarry Street. The teacher, Miss Anne, was in charge, scaring us all with her punishment of being taken to a really dark room and left there for hours, eventually, after a few months Mywo took me away.

There was this old man, Mr Mullrin, living in our street, coming back late one night with a flambeau in one hand and a bottle of rum in the other, he stumbled and fell, catching himself alight, alarmed, people seeing the blaze thought it was a 'Sucunair' (vampire) and started to beat the poor man and only when someone recognised him did they stopped and threw cold water on his poor body, which actually killed him.

Folks, then, were very superstitious!

At the junction of Laventille Hill Road and Ovid Alley, 300 yards from our house, lived my aunts and uncles, the Bowen family on my mother side, the five sisters and brothers, shared a house, Daisy, Cecile, Sydney, Clara, Edna and Dewdrops, they also had a Tamboo Bamboo band. My uncle Sydney also practised Shango in a tent up the Laventille Hills, we could hear the beating of the drums from our house…

My mother's boyfriend at the time was Clifford Persil who had come to live with us, his mother, Hortense, performed at Shango ceremonies. Once when visiting us she heard the sound of the Shango drums coming from the hills, her eyes wide open she explained to my mother that the drums were calling her… Mywo then asked me to take Hortense to Uncle Sydney at the Shango ceremony, so, holding her hand climbing the hills, we followed the sound of the drums. When approaching the tent, she suddenly stopped and turned to me saying that she was catching the power and started to stumble, waving her hands above her head, eyes lost in another sphere, she hissed and kicked, frightening the hell out of me and, leaving her there, I ran down the hills as fast as I could, not looking back once. Eventually Mywo went to get her."

Shango

Shango is an African religion that might have originated in south west Africa. Shango, was the deity of the Yoruba people and the devotees of a Shango cult might call themselves 'Yoruba' but apart from Trinidad, Shango/Orisha, 'God of Thunder, is venerated in Haiti, Brazil, Cuba, Venezuela, Porto Rico among others... he is portrayed with a double axe on his three heads, the holy colours are white and red.

"I have heard from people who actually have been to a Shango ceremony and have witnessed the power manifesting itself upon a person, that his dancing or swaying rapidly becomes more frantic, he then starts shaking his shoulders and throws himself on the floor, speaking an unknown language.

My friend Irwin was once a spectator at such a ceremony, looking at the woman in trance, he whispered to the friend he was with that it seemed that the woman was pregnant, with the sound of the drums, the singing and clapping and the distance between them, in no way, says Irwin, could she have heard such a whisper, let alone ever noticed Irwin amongst all the crowd. After a while, still in a trance she moved closer and closer to Irwin and told him to mind his own business. He stood there totally bewildered, then gathering his composure, hurried out of the tent.

I suppose that it cannot be logically explained, only feel how the mind interact with hidden forces in the universe, that no-one can rationally translate or explain with words. Paranormal?

Hortense had four sons, Toto, Chaufer, Angelo and Clifford and two daughters, Baby and Carmen. The rather feminine Angelo, owned a dry cleaning business in Prince Street where I would go with my mother who, sitting me on the counter, would urge me to sing the calypso songs I had picked up by accompanying her to the calypso tents. My repertoire was quite rich. I must have been about five years old.

Tamboo Bamboo

My uncles and aunts had a Tamboo Bamboo band; to turn bamboos into musical instruments, you had, at a certain time of the year and according to the moon, to harvest the bamboo green and put it to dry in the sun until it has turned yellow. If not cut at the right time the insects will reduce it to powder. The bamboos would then be cut into varying lengths and hollowed to get different pitches; for the bass, called boom, a larger five feet long bamboo was required, it would be stamped on the ground. In a marching band the bass player had to walk with his legs well apart to avoid the bamboo to fall on his toes, which caused many injuries.

For a higher pitch tone two shorter bamboos would be held upright and beat against each other. The highest pitch tone bamboo would be thinner and shorter and struck with a stick.

People experimented all possibilities to acquire different sounds, gin bottles half filled with different level of water to produce variances, also struck with a spoon and later on replaced by a steel hub. None of these instruments played melodies, it was a background rhythm for the singing choruses, the 'Chantwells'.

"One of the songs my family Tamboo Bamboo band sang went like that:

Don' t break up my band
If you break up my band
Its war and rebellion
Don't break up my band
If you break up my band
I'll live in the station

This song was aimed at the police and rival bands, there were so many clashes between the bands and naturally with the police. Stick fighting was associated with Tamboo Bamboo bands and also a very popular game with the common folks, a game that sometimes became real and bloody.

The Tamboo Bamboo band would also play during the fights assisted by a Chantwell who would sing, cheering on the stick fighters. Originally these Chantwell were women preserving the tribe history and gradually were replaced by men.

Chantwells

The 'Chantwell' was a singer, a soloist really, who also could acted as a historian, narrating, informing people not only of present events, but past epics, genealogies, (like the African Griot who could narrate stories centuries old) It was the birth of the Calypso in a way and a way for oppressed people to spread their opinion about without others to understand, especially when French Creole (patois) was the dominant language. The Chantwell sang for all sorts of occasions like for wakes, stick fighting or during carnival.

At stick-fighting, the Chantwell addressed the crowd, singing stories, boosting the fighters in ring. I remember a chant going like this: "When ah dead bury ma clothes, Ah don want your sweet man to wear my clothes, when ah dead..." repeated over and over during the stick fight.

Stick fighters were usually seen marching in front of the Tamboo Bamboo bands, protecting them from the eventual confrontation with other bands, singing: "Tell them tell them we aint fraid nobody, wywywywywywywy...tell them tell them…" When the clashes of bands occurred the bamboos were used as weapons and when split they caused dangerous wounds.

Stick fighting

Stick fighting is a kind of martial art in some countries, still practised in the martial art communities in many parts of the world. It is said that the Trinidadians had inherited it from the Africans, the Spanish and the French who named it 'Calinda' or 'Kalenda'.

In Trinidad, its origins go back to the 18th century when stick fighting was practised as a dance, you had two men in a circle, formed by people betting for the champion and a 'Chantwell' will sing a story inciting the two fighters into the fight.

It sometimes was to defend one's territory.

"When it was time for my uncles and aunts to cut the bamboos up in Trou Macaque, (an area up on the Laventille hills) I will sneak out of the house and follow them, when seeing me they will chase me and I, pretending to leave, would come back hiding along the way. They eventually came to terms with my determination and let me help in dragging the bamboos back to a tent in Ovid Alley.

The Monday before lent was the start of the carnival with 'j'Ouvert' morning, the official opening time for the bands, to play, if I remember correctly, was 5 am but at 4 am one could already hear the Tamboo Bamboo bands heading higher on the hills to Trou Macaque where the police would not dare to go.

By 5 am they would come down through Laventille Road to the town with the followers that had gathered along the way, all disguised in rags, blowing into hosepipes and beating steel shovel on their shoulders, or brandishing tree branches over their heads, wearing papier mache face masks.

Lying in bed awake, long before time, I would try to escape from the room where I and Stella slept, my mother in the dark, sensing my stirring on the floor, would just grab me, urging me to go back to sleep. I would wait, lying perfectly still, pretending to fall asleep, then, when a more regular sound of her breathing indicated that she had fallen back to sleep, I would creep out gently taking my time, aware of any movement Stella would make. Finally out of the house, I would run out in the dark night to meet the band with just a vest on and would go all the way to town with them and beat some small bamboos, collecting the money given by the people at seeing such a small boy.

Later on that morning when my mother eventually met up with the band, spotting me on one of my uncles' shoulders too tired to walk any longer, I would see her raising her arms in the air, shouting from afar:

"Look at that, the boy ran away with no pants and nothing to eat!"

She would then drag me back home, give me breakfast and dress me in a costume to join the children's carnival."

CHAPTER II
From Ovid Alley to Nepaul Street

Sterling's brother, Herman, takes his daily exercise by taking the fifteen minute walk that separates his house from Sterling's.

His small and slight frame project an amazingly youthful air and the way he carries himself, as if he never has a worry in the world contribute to doubt his 86 years.

He often ends his sentences with a giggle or laughter as if to cancel the seriousness of his words. He was brought up with his sister Sheila, by their great grandmother who lived 'down the Laventille hill' in Success Village, while Sterling remained in Ovid Alley 'up the hill' with Mywo. Sunday school provided an occasion for the children to enjoy being reunited for games and play.

The three children have inherited some of Mywo's way of approaching life, a combination of their ancestor's vital balance with the cosmos, frank and innocent virtues and a naturally simple contentment.

She was a formidable woman with a strong identity, a leader, a fighter and a strong believer and, despite all the years of hardship she had encountered, had retained an immense compassion and genuine understanding for her fellow men. Her kindness and generosity was free of all expectations and there was never any questioning or prying. Her laughter could be heard from afar, it was deep and contagious and so was her fury!

"What! If you had heard her when someone cheesed her off, she could be a pretty merciless adversary, verbally and physically, but she rarely lost her temper unnecessarily, she was very true to herself, her straightforwardness made you aware soon enough where you stood, she would not take on any nonsense, or foolishness, there was so much wisdom in the way she embraced the good and the bad alike, the bitter and the sweet.

I cannot remember why I ended up living with my father for few months, but obviously, Mywo had good reasons for sending me away but I tend to believe that he wanted his children with him only to suit his own interest.

He lived with his girlfriend who was terribly rough with me, beating me and punishing me all the time without any apparent reason, she obviously resented my being there. When eventually Mywo heard of this, she took me away from him and sent me to my godmother who was nicknamed Queen.

Queen, a tall and dark Tobagonian, lived with her husband, Philip, in a large house (it was for me at the time) at 67 Gloster Lodge Road, Belmont, a different class area south east of Port of Spain, at the foot of Laventille Hills.

There were sitting dinners with proper cutlery, the china teapot had a cosy, I was told how to lay the table and to sit at meals. I was learning and observing unfamiliar ways and eventually ended like a little servant.

I would be sent to the market to do the shopping, which during the war and food restriction was very helpful as I attracted the vendor's sympathy and brought home more groceries than expected.

I attended the Gloster Lodge Moravian school where every morning the children who, considered malnourished, received a pint of milk."

I sometimes get impatient when the necessity arises for me to go further into the emotional side of a story, to bring out what Sterling might have felt at relevantly sensitive moments of his life, as a child in the world of misbehaved adults.

Most of the time my questions are met with reluctance and impatience, it precipitates Sterling to take a pose, head downcast, his hand rubbing his forehead, a characteristic that I became very familiar with but also indicate that I should change direction. In these moments, the courage to pry for any more details fails me. I feel like a torturer, incessantly delving, never satisfied with his succinct answers and incapacity at going into more elaborated reactions and at describing his inner thoughts.

He treats emotions and feelings with dismissal and a wave of his hand.

In the year that I intermittently sat with him for the purpose of this book, waiting for the memories to resurface again after having been for so long buried into a deliberate oblivion, I comprehended how wrong I was to think that I would manage to expose his profound thoughts, never finding out if it was in order to protect himself or out of the incapability for him to acknowledge or describe past anguish or just simple emotions.

Is the need to raise more than the facts, really necessary, aren't there enough signs to grasp the essence of a human being? Shouldn't I be content with just the stories?

Finally, I asked him if he remembered friends he might have made at the Moravian school.

" I had few friends at school and most of the time, when at home, I played alone at the back of the house, flying kites, spinning top or playing with marbles, it seems that I never search for friends, I was very shy.

In the early 60s, I would be reunited in London with two friends from the Moravian school, who had recently arrived in the UK:

Frank Superville, a brilliant athlete, came to the UK to become an engineer for BT and also represented them in sport, winning many trophies as a sprinter. He eventually moved back to Trinidad in 1979. My other friend from school was Horace Sampson, whom I saw again in London when on his way to Austria to study medicine.

Before his departure I gave him a couple of drums I had made for him to take to the university he had enrolled in, with the idea that he could introduce steel band there.

Only in the early 90s was I to meet him again by chance when a gig took me to Graz (Austria), and was happily surprised after the concert, to see Horace walking into our dressing room.

Later on over dinner I was to hear how, after becoming a doctor, he had moved to a practice in Graz and how with the drums I had given him he had taught the students at university and formed a little band."

After having made an arrangement to meet Sterling later on that week and not finding him at home, I, slightly frustrated, waited in his front garden when one of his neighbours, whom I had seen passing by the gate a couple of times before, directed me to the betting shop at the corner of the road. I understood that either Sterling was well known in the street therefore his whereabouts, or that his afternoon habits had become a well-known fact.

There in the shop, I saw a very concentrated Sterling, totally absorbed and focused on the horses racing across the screen. Twice I had to draw his attention and when finally he acknowledged my presence it was with such a broad and friendly smile that I had already forgotten the waiting outside his front door.

Silently walking back to his house, his head bent, it felt as if I was leading him to some excruciating torture.

Asking him how long he had entertained this hobby, sheepishly he answered that now and then he got drawn to it, more so now as he was not so busy.

I wondered if he had forgotten all about our meeting, he replied shaking his head, "No no no, I would have eventually come back!"

I wondered how long I would have had to wait. I also became familiar with his famous "No.no.no!"

He then made two cups of tea, bringing out lemon biscuits and madeleines, we sat at the large kitchen table disturbing 'Minette', the impressive white and brown/orange cat curled up on one of the armchairs, the afternoon light playing on the copper pots hanging on the wall.

After having told me that 'Minette' was a rescued cat from France, Sterling is now pressing me to get on with the story, in a hurry it seems to get rid of me and without any warning, his sharp memory recalled our last encounter and the question I had asked earlier in the week when the telephone had interrupted and stopped us going any further:

" Last time, I remember you asked me about my father, well, I have to tell you about how he one day appeared at Queen with the excuse of taking me out for the day, Queen could not refuse nor had time to find my mother to ask her permission, he was my father after all.

He took me to his sister's house in Four Road and left me there. He then went to my great grand where my sister Sheila and Herman were living and brought them back to Four Road as well. We were there just long enough for Queen, when the time for my return had passed, to find my mother and inform her that Edwin had not brought me back.

I got told that Mywo got into a rage and charged into his house in Belmont , bypassing everyone standing in her way, taking my father by his shirt, shook him and pushed him about regardless his protestation and his threats of never finding us. Mywo went searching for us in all the places he might have taken us. She was not more successful at his sister's house, as we had been already taken over garden fences onto another location.

It was only few days later that Mywo heard that we had been spotted at Edwin' sister and, not caring at being seen or heard losing her temper, frightened the life out of the sister who eventually had no choice but to let us go.

My father had not kidnapped us for the love of us as he was avoiding having to pay maintenance to my mother.

I went back to Queen, my brother and sister to great grand.

You see, in Trinidad and probably in most of the Caribbean islands, the children were often brought up by their grandparents or close relatives while the parents had to fend hard for a living and did not always have space and time to care for their own, and as often was the case, families consisted of many children!

I stayed at Queen four years."

I was surprised when I asked how he would describe these four years at Queen, he admitted at only remembering the unhappy time there but did not think it interesting enough to talk about it.

We then talked about remembering certain incidents from our childhood that had a great significance, how the happy memories, the shocking or hurtful ones have shaped some of our behaviour and pattern in relationship to others and as children, made an enormous impact on our future beings and how we would raise our own children.

Sterling gets very adamant when pointing out that then, there was the adult world in which children obeyed and that was that!

Finally, after another diversion, he brings out another story not convinced that it was interesting enough to tell:

"On a Sunday when my godmother and her husband attended the evening church service, I went to play with the nearby children and when involved in a game I would often forget all sense of time.

I came home to find out that all the doors had been locked and after knocking a few times, I understood that they would not let me in, so I just sat on the back stairs waited all night there and when morning came, I got up and watered the plants as I usually was asked to do, as if nothing had happened

On another occasion of being late, Queen, said that she needed to get the bad blood out of me and with these words hit me on the head with a stone, naturally I bled profusely. When her husband came home and enquired about the wound on my head, a terrible argument ensued, to end by Philip summoning his wife to take me home to my mother or there will be no end to her troubles. But she didn't and in return got hit by her husband.

They had a dog, called Rex, who was my little friend.

One morning Rex followed me to the market, I kept chasing him back knowing all too well that he was not allowed to stray too far away from the house. Despite my attempts at chasing him back he would just turn around and persist in coming after me, staying at some distance behind, until I gave up.

From time to time, I would glance back at him seeing him stop abruptly, as if he pretended not having moved at all! He escorted me so during the two miles to the market, playing that game every time I turned back to look at him, then in the busy market amongst all I totally lost sight of him. On my return home, without Rex, naturally I was questioned what I had done with the dog as neighbours had reported seeing me with Rex.

I can still hear Queen's voice:

"You go and find him and if you don't, don't bother ever coming back."

For years I had been waiting to hear this and this was too much of an opportunity to miss, I then hurried to my mother's in Nepaul Street, St James, where she had moved to.

You see I never spoke to Mywo of the bad treatment I sometimes received from Queen, to spare her from worrying about me and for not causing any confusion, knowing perfectly well that by telling my mother, she would most likely have given Queen a far worse feedback than the one I had received.

Until then she had believed that Queen's environment offered an opportunity for me to acquire a 'better' upbringing, if told of the cruel treatment I was receiving, she surely would have taken me away from Gloster Lodge Road long time ago.

After this last incident Mywo kept me with her.

Few days later, Queen's husband came to Nepaul Street to inform us that Rex had returned, that all was well now and that he came to bring me back to Gloster Lodge Road.

Mywo's words were few but to the point, "The child does not want to go back and I shall respect his wish."

My godfather: "Do you mean that this child is going to live in a shack like this while we can offer him a better way of living?"

"That has nothing to do with it and what has happened, such is his decision."

He left totally bemused.

Chapter III
ST JAMES, 1940
The origins of Pans/ Tripoli/ Hell's Kitchen

Mywo registered me in St Crispin's school in Woodbrook and I happily shared 'the shack' where Clifford and her lived in Nepaul Street, St James.

Clifford, was a tall, fair skinned, man with straight features, inherited from his Carib descent, he worked at the Port of Spain wharfs and gambled, often taking trips deep into the heart of the countryside to meet other gambling enthusiasts.

Sheila and Herman came to live with us and we all squeezed in the tiny place, it felt good to be all united, it felt really secure and I perceived this period of my childhood as one of the happiest.

I joined a football team 'The Greens' for which Stella made our football shirts, white with a green V in satin on the front and back of the t-shirts. Like most schools, we had a cricket team and when we entered the competition with 'The Tranquillity Boys School'. I made top score, 61 runs not out and won my school a cup and sixpence for myself that the delighted headmaster, Mr Dolly, announced after the tournament. I was too shy to go to his office to claim my prize and never collected the sixpence that would have been most welcomed.

I made a few friends at St Crispin, one of them Irwin Clement, who after having lived in London in the 50s, went to America for twenty-four years and now shares his time between London and Tobago."

Clement recalled that Sterling was very popular at school, "That somehow, you noticed him, he had a distinctive way of keeping a distance from the other boys, it is hard to explain, but without doing much, people were drawn to him and when he laughed it was with his whole body, he also excelled at all sports, another reason for all the boys to look up to him."

"1940 was the year when I really started to toy with paint pans, biscuit tins and any other metal pans.

We were all searching for new notes.

I already have spoken about my family Tamboo Bamboo band and of the gin bottles beaten with a spoon and the steel hub, gradually, I cannot say a date for sure but according to the record it must have been late 30s, between 1937 and 1941, when empty tin containers, biscuit tins and paint pans were integrated into the Tamboo Bamboo bands.

At first the biscuit tin replaced the bamboo bass, which often fell on the players toes.

The paint tin had no notes, by beating it constantly the dents gave different sounds and soon the players realised the possibility to obtain various tones, later on it was called the Ping Pong drum, held in one hand and played with one stick.

From one tone to two then to three, a melody could be played on the paint pan, ('Ping Pong' because of the sound that came from it), the first melody executed was a nursery rhyme 'Mary had a little lamb', the notes were C, D, E. Later in the 50s it was renamed the Tenor pan.

When tuners first experimented with the paint pan, in order to bring out the notes, they realised that sinking the top of the pan was far more practical than sinking it from the convex side, giving it also a better tonal quality,

The Ping Pong, or Tenor pan, plays the melody and has most notes, over the years it evolved to about thirty-six notes on a specially made oversized drum.

Metal containers were well sought after everywhere in POS, in the new harbour construction site where empty cement drums would be taken from, at the biscuit factory and the scrap yards, dustbins from residents homes were also stolen which resulted in having them chained to whatever anchor...

Of course these discoveries were challenging and travelled rapidly around the island, players were trying to outdo each other in their search for more notes and formed groups of different neighbourhoods, I must say of rival neighbourhoods!

Alexander Rag Time Tamboo Bamboo band from Newtown Woodbrook, was the first to incorporate steel instruments to a bamboo band such as the paint and biscuit tins, I was about nine years old when I first saw and heard this band in a barrack's yard in Prince Street, the band was playing for a Bamboo Band competition, they were about twenty players, very few bamboos, the major sound came from the tin pans, biscuit drums and steel hubs, since these instruments had no notes the melody was sang.

I stood there in awe, looking and admiring the bandmaster standing tall and grand in his scissor tail coat and top hat, conducting the band with a baton in his hands, it also was the first time a bandmaster was conducting a bamboo band.

They were singing:

"Run you run Kaiser William
Run you run
Run you run Kaiser William
Run you run
Hear what Chamberlain says (stop)
Cheer boys cheer (stop)
With charity and prosperity
We'll conquer Germany

The abrupt stop in the song was a new innovation in singing arrangement.

A year later all bamboos were removed from the bands and put aside in favour of the paint pan and biscuit tin.

The steel drum was at first a percussion instrument and gradually, over the years, it developed to became a melodic instrument as new notes were discovered on the Ping Pong, then a larger drum was required and by 1945 the steel pan men realised that by using the 25 gallons sweet oil drum, the coconut oil drum, they could bring out five and six notes, that drum was named the Kittle drum and it could play the melody.

The Kittle drum was strapped over the shoulder and played with two sticks.

From the bare sticks, players realised that by covering the end of the sticks with rubber it made a less metallic sound and brought out a more accurate musical tone.

At the same time as the five notes 'Ping Pong' a two notes drum called 'The Dudup' was brought in, then came the 55 gallons petrol drum tuned to eight to ten notes, as the experiment went on many more tunes were played.

For sinking the 55 gallon drum a sledge hammer will be utilized and at times a cannon ball.

The notes were grooved with a steel punch, each segment was grooved into the number desired, then tuned by knocking within the segments until the right note emerged, large section meant a low tone, a small segment a higher pitch.

As a bass we used the light caustic soda drum to bring out four and five notes, the first band we saw with this caustic soda drum was 'Southern Symphony' led by Belgrave Bonaparte.

You can easily imagine the impact these discoveries made on the pan men, and the excitement with which they were received, every musician from Trinidad to Tobago was experimenting, I have to name some of these men even if many other escape my memory.

We all know that a discovery or achievement in any field is the result of many participants and that many have remained unrecognised.

Belgrave Bonaparte from Southern Symphony
Hugh Borde , Hell's Kitchen
Andrew Delabastide, Crusaders

Neville Jules from 'Hellyard' band
Ellie Manette, Invaders
Sonny Roach, Sun Valley
Grandville Sealey, and I with Tripoli
Duddley Smith, Rising Sun
Winston Spree Simon from Tokyo to Fascinators
Theodore Stevens, Southern All Stars to Free French
Philmore Boots Davidson   Casablanca
Ziglee Constantine   Bar 20
Anthony Williams, North Stars

The 55 gallons drum was also used for a three notes drum called 'The Balay', named so in west Port of Spain, in central POS it had a different name 'The Grundig', in the south some other name was given but wherever it came from, the drum had the same deep tones.

When the ' Biscuit Tin' was given notes it became 'The Tune Boom', named so by Neville Jules who was the first to give it four notes.

By 1949/50 the Ping Pong had gained twenty-one notes!

It was in 1942 that Sterling's involvement with the steel drums became an important factor in his life, first with Tripoli (the name was taken from the film *The Shores of Tripoli*) and with the youth band, Hell's Kitchen.

"Tripoli's pan yard, was in Ethell Street, in a bamboo shack near the sea, we called it the shores of Tripoli and whistled the marine hymn of that name. At Carnival we performed drills like the marines, marched singing the hymn. The 'pan yards' were really the home of all steel band men, a place where all drums would be kept, a meeting place for all players and steel band enthusiasts.

Hell's Kitchen was in Carl and Hugh Borde's back yard, in a gateway off St James main road and Brunton Street. Their father had a drugstore just up the road from where we lived, so I would hang around there with some other boys, Clement was one of them, we would pop in and lime with them always on the look-out, afraid of being spotted by a member of our family, you see, steel bands had a very bad reputation then, always associated with violence and their members as hoodlums.

Tripoli was no exception and was regarded as a band where mothers would not have liked their children to hang about with.

The players were all in their late teens, while we, Carl and Hugh Borde and other boys were just teenagers, so independently of Tripoli, we formed a youth band ' Hell's Kitchen', we were eight boys and one girl, Cynthia.

Cynthia Davies, seemed to have a natural predisposition with the pan, she also excelled in all sports, particularly at cricket and football. We used to hang out together."

Sterling perceived my sudden interest in Cynthia and with a wave of his hand dismissed my curiosity.

"I was not interested in girls at all, Cynthia and I hung out together like school mates, as friends, I certainly do not remember having had a crush on her, or any other girls at that stage, my mind was not set that way, my interests were sports and music.

My spare time was spent tuning and playing, getting together with the other boys who were in the band.

In 1945, VE day, Irwin joined us to play on a truck during the celebration under 'the supervision' of our mothers, who consumed a considerable amount of Robinson Crusoe's rum and were there more for the fun of it than keeping an eye on us. We were the first steel band to be sponsored by Robinson Crusoe rum company, the picture on the rum bottle was of a man with a parrot on his shoulder and so was the man seating on the top of our truck, dressed in a Robinson Crusoe outfit made of coconut leaves, holding an umbrella with a live parrot on his shoulder.

We played with the paint pan, the biscuit drum, the steel hub and the Dudup.

We used to experiment tuning small drums as the big steel pan was a late discovered in 1946, we spent more time tuning drums than we did with our schoolwork.

At the school roll, first thing in the morning, before the class started, the teacher would call my name and someone in the classroom would then shout, "He under the Downs tree tuning pans Sir!"

So when I finally showed up, making some excuse for being late, the teacher, Arnotte Joseph, would ask me to show my hands, naturally dirty from pan tuning.

Tripoli band leader, Joe Crick, would at carnival dress as a Nazi, he was nicknamed 'The Fuhrer'. Well known to be an excellent fighter, I remember him challenging Invaders members (another band) that he could fight two of their men without weapons, 'Invaders' declined without hesitation!

After four years with 'Hell's Kitchen', as I was getting older, I gradually got more involved with Tripoli, Granville Sealey, older than I, was the official pan tuner for the band and when I also started to tune he took a dislike of me, which was accentuated even more when the rumour passed around that I was a better tuner than him.

At the after carnival party in 1946, when, as the tradition goes, all the players and mass paraders get together to celebrate, Granville, slightly drunk came to me with a drink:

"Have a drink Stywo"! (knowing very well that I did not drink).

"No thanks," replied I

"Well if you don't want to drink it then wear it !" and joining the words with action, threw it in my face and all over my shirt before I could even react, so surprised was I at his behaviour.

I got into such a rage that two of my friends had to hold me back to prevent me from getting into a fight. That same evening with seven of us, we decided to leave Tripoli and form our own band.

So, Coya Menard, Eman and Roger Thorpe, Red Mike, Eric Drayton, Cyril Jackman and I, formed 'Crossfire'. We were searching for a suitable name for our band when the Rialto cinema in St James was screening *Crossfire* a film starring Robert Mitchum, it inspired us to give our band that name.

People enjoyed spending time at the movies, mostly American films were shown then, war movies and westerns were a favourite amongst pan men. Most steel bands were named after films, for instance, Casablanca, Invaders, Desperadoes, Tokyo, and many others.

We all know how cinema has an enormous influence on opening our way of thinking, bringing new horizons to our lives, new ideas and escapism, I suppose even more at that time in Trinidad!

The way the films pictured different worlds, life styles, romances, warfare, fashion became a source of inspiration to many of us, the most determined even adopted ways of dressing, attitudes and words.

Earlier Irwin and his family had moved to Belmont, an area too far away for him to keep up with our band in St James, so now and then he played with a local band there, 'Rising Sun' in Valley Road, the Chinese Savannah, always hiding and keeping his eyes where his father would appear, cycling back from work, making sure not to be spotted, he would then run home as fast as he could to arrive before him.

Later on, he was allowed to play congo drums for the Starlight Variety Show with the Pearl Primus dance group in Guyana.

He eventually joined 'Demboys' steel band."

Sterling's departure from Tripoli had not been as easy as he thought he might have anticipated, Joe Crick got so annoyed with them leaving and forming a new band, that he decided to hold a 'smear campaign', saying that all members who had left were faggots, a connotation that in Trinidad, where macho was the norm, to be called a faggot was the worst insult you could get.

"We did not take much notice and tried to ignore whoever called us names, we were so excited about forming our band that it took our mind off any negative predicament.

More players from Tripoli left the band, such as Makfield who worked at Shell Company and who organized for our new band to purchase a dozen oil drums at a very good price.

We established our pan yard in Hyderabad Street, St James, in Cyril Jackman's yard, a quarter of a mile from Tripoli.

Cyril Jackman's house had enough space underneath to store the drums that I made for our band. I was there every day, making tuning with some of our Crossfire members, Eman and Roger Thorp, Sam & Rudolph Bodoo, Eric Drayton, who lived opposite, and Cyril Jackman in charge of the band.

The responsibility to be captain of a band was not a role I would have enjoyed taking on as, when problems with the players occurred, police will always be involved and the captain had to answer for all disputes."

And disputes were not in Sterling's vocabulary, either because he hated confrontation out of this immense need he has for peace and quiet, or would not have known how to deal with it out of fear where an inner violence might lead him.

"Eman Thorpe was about three years younger than me, undisciplined and well known for causing havoc wherever he went, a talented pan musician with a promising future. When I left the band in 1951, he became Crossfire pan tuner with

Kelvin "Zuzie" Saint Rose. He also was very talented at throwing stones at the police and eventually ended in court. He booked a return ticket to Barbados on a ship sailing to England, at the stopover in Barbados he stayed on the ship, hiding for the long journey to the UK.

Funny enough when in 1956, he arrived in Victoria I greeted him and gave him hospitality in Ashmore Road, Queens Park."

Chapter IV
A picnic at Fort George

"The ban on carnival that had been in effect since the beginning of the war, was then lifted, but streets parades of any sort were still forbidden outside the festival.

In 1947, at Easter time, despite the interdiction, we all decided to take our drums and a picnic up to the hills of Port of Spain, to the Fort George fortifications."

Fort George was built by the British in 1804 to protect the island and the harbour from a possible invasion. Towering 1000 feet over the western side of the capital and the harbour, fifteen minutes away from the city of POS, Fort George with its natural environment is a peace haven where to escape the heat of the town and just sit there contemplating in the fresh breeze, gazing at the view over the Caroni swamps, the harbour and far out to the sea, with your thoughts gliding in tune with the birds in the sky.

Funny enough, the Victorian house built there in late 19th century, as a signal point, was designed by the son of a West African king!

"We left our pan yard walking and already playing, with our drums around the neck, our friends and family following, all knowing perfectly well that playing in the streets outside carnival was forbidden, naturally, Stella was with the party, never would she have missed an afternoon of music and entertainment! For this occasion we all wore white shirts, white flannel pants, white shoes and a red beret, taking all the small back roads to avoid being seen by the police, with only one main road to cross.

The afternoon was filled with music, dance, and laughter.

On our way back late that day, walking though the same roads, still playing and gathering along the way people who, when approaching the main road crossing had become a crowd.

The police also joined in but with a different motive; a British inspector driving on the same main road and seeing the crowd drove to St James police station sending some men to deal with us.

We were almost home, when walking at the side of the burial ground wall, two police vans finally caught up with us, policemen running out of their vehicle with batons and bull pistol in their hands, shouting, "STOP POLICE RAID."

The drums around our neck came out so fast, flying over the cemetery wall, with us running as if we had seen a spirit rising from the graves, when seeing the police chasing us, people from the nearby houses came out with wooden sticks, ordering the police to leave us alone being so close to home.

The drums dropped on the side of the road were taken to the police station by the officers but none in the burial ground were found.

We waited until daylight to pick up our drums from the cemetery but all the others were only recovered later, after having sat in the police station back yard for a few months in rain and sun. Through a member of our mass band who was the son of a sergeant at that station, did we finally get to collect the drums, by then pretty rusty."

Chapter V
Chaguaramas

The Americans arrived in Trinidad in 1940 on the *USS St Louis* to establish their base in Chaguaramas, south of Port of Spain.

The British government had leased the region to the American's for ninety-nine years in exchange for destroyers that had long seen better days but contrary to what people believed, the base was not for the protection of Trinidad but for America to have a stronghold on an island near South America and to control the Nazi U boats patrolling the islands coastline.

All the villagers living in the area were evicted, families had to find new homes, the bathing beaches and beach club had become inaccessible to all and in the villages all homes were demolished.

Air and naval army bases were erected and submarines were stationed in Tetron Bay. The Waller and Carlsen airstrips were established and in Mucurapo, a district northeast of POS centre, an airfield was created. In Tobago, an emergency airstrip was also set up.

In 1943, the US sent US nationals, Puerto Ricans, to replace the black American soldiers to avoid conflicts between the black Americans and the local population but the clashes remained as the Puerto Ricans who were stationed in Mucurapo, considered themselves white.

In 1943/44 Chaguaramas had become a military base and all the soldiers, sailors and pilots were seen in the street of Port of Spain. Their arrival made a very deep impact on the life of the Trinidadians and if the results had not altogether been beneficial, it had procured jobs with better wages than the local employment, wages that had not been seen before. Consequently a considerable amount of people came to Port of Spain from rural areas, from Tobago and other islands.

Not so beneficial was the presence of the Americans as it contributed in the dramatic rise in prostitution, it increased the number of Trinidadian women making their living as prostitutes with American soldiers who hung around the streets of Port of Spain, especially in the bars in Charlotte Street where prostitutes and pimps were usually seen.

Gilda was a famous bar and meeting point for Americans and Calypsonians alike, Dirty Jim Swizzle Club in South Quay, opposite the station was another well-known spot, bars and night clubs were full until morning.

The city centre was exploding with night life, in this atmosphere quarrels and fights were a common occurrence.

Mothers, daughters, girls, who had been seen as 'respectable' were taking to the streets and, as a consequence, triggered the rise of the pimps called, Saga Boys or sweet men, because of their fancy way of dressing.

"They wore baggy trousers, 16 inch bottom, 32 inch knees, imitating the way the singer and actor, Cab Calloway, was dressed in a film, shirts with upturned cuffs and two handkerchiefs hung from their trousers back pockets, they wore a felt hat or a Stetson with feathers on one side and two-tone shoes. They were big gamblers mostly involved in dice games.

Some pan men led the lives of Saga Boys but usually a real involvement with pans did not give you enough time to pursue other assignments.

The Calypsonian Rupert Grant known under the stage name as Lord Invader, caricatured the era in his song:

" Rum and Cocacola"

"Everyone knows this song : (Sterling singing it and tapping the rhythm on the table)

Since the Yankee come to Trinidad
They got the young girls all goin'mad
Young girls say they treat 'em nice
Make Trinidad like paradise

The fights of American soldiers were famous for their racially based violence, verbal or physical abuses and drunkenness that would, when an appropriate time occurred, bring the Trinidadians to follow the sailors and rob them of their clothes while they were in the bushes with girls, the opportunity for revenge was always close at hand.

The sailor's hat was well sought after by the steel band men for their masquerades and often, when walking down the street, a hat would be snatched from a sailor's head, giving him no time to see where the thief or hat had gone to, so swift and fast were thieves.

Once in a rum shop, in St James, a sailor was beaten by the locals, trucks of American sailors armed with baseball bats and other weapons arrived, raiding the whole area and closing it down, well after everyone had already decamped, so prompt were the residents at disappearing. Not a soul was to be found as all houses were suddenly locked, windows, where people had once been seen, had their shutters closed and there was no one around to give any information.

There were many similar incidents between Americans and locals.

The presence of the considerable number of sailors on the island might have contributed to the appeal the sailor costume had on the mass players, a masquerade that became a favourite for years to come."

Fancy Sailor costume has been Sterling's choice for his many appearances at Notting Hill's carnival, always reviving its origins.

Masquerades representing American sailors in the POS carnivals became common, parodying and mimicking their ways, dressed with bellbottom trousers, sailor jumper and hat, recreating wartime scenes and bad behaviour…

When the Americans gave parties, invitations were often sent to all the local girls to attend one of these dancing events at the American base, trucks were sent to pick them up and bring them back, sometimes in the early hours of the morning.

In September 1942, a Guardian article advertised these kind of events:

Monos party on Sunday:

The girls who are going to Monos island for the all day party on Sunday are reminded that they must be at the USO club before 10am. Where Army trucks will be waiting to carry them to the boat. Slacks or shorts may be worn for the out-trip, but the hostesses request that the girls take a short dress for the dance in the evening, as they did for the Green Hill entertainment, also bring along a plate and a fork. There will be swimming, lunch and dancing with dinner in between, and the men are looking forward to entertaining the girls so don't disappoint them.

"I would, on some similar occasion, see Stella dressing up, her cousins arriving to meet her, all looking very handsome.

Once Stella took me with her to one of these parties where I was given hot dogs and coca cola and then taken to a dormitory where I slept the night until my mother was ready to go home."

At the end of the war, many local girls left the islands with their American soldiers and from the stories they all had heard about the United States, they pictured it as a sort of Eldorado and an amazing opportunity for them to leave the islands and its uncertain future. Little did they know that they were actually heading to the heart of economic exploitation, which, was not going to provide a rapid resolution for that generation of women.

Carnival and music bands were prohibited from the streets of POS from 1941 to the end of the war, except for those who took refuge in the East Dry River.

The East Dry River divides Port of Spain between east and west. During the dry season, after the water had evaporated, it was used as a road where the steel bands paraded and performed mass during carnival time, Mardi Gras.

People from town would never come up or cross the Dry River, it was far too dangerous knowing it to be the domain of gang warfare, the fights between the bands were numerous, often caused by the adversity and rivalry between the players, the ability in playing, the quality of the drums, the tunes chosen, the area they came from and very often girls!!!

Despite the carnival ban, the mass bands and steel band players could carry on in the East Dry River without fear of a police irruption.

"Since the age of ten, I had been so involved in making, tuning, and playing pan, that my schoolwork had suffered badly and gradually became non-existent.

My friend, Irwin, who was not to be seen near pans, would come to my back yard and join me in playing and tuning, when time was up for him to go home, Mywo would just stand there with her hand on her hip, one word sufficed for Irwin to stop whatever he was doing and to get up without any hesitation:

"Irwin"?

Irwin knew well enough that my mother was not someone to repeat an order twice, she would stand on the steps outside with her hand still on her hip watching Irwin walking away and making sure he was not diverting from his way home for she knew that Irwin would pass Hugh Borde's house where we often stopped by. Irwin would glance back few times seeing her from the distance standing there at the same spot, looking and waiting for him to disappear from her sight.

The way my mother called his name and the sight of her on those steps has left a deep and memorable impression on Irwin's memory for I have heard him evocating it many times.

At the end of the school term, when the class results were displayed on the blackboard and that my name written at the bottom of the list demonstrated to my shame, how badly I had done, I decided that I will not be so humiliated the following term and studied.

My determination convinced my mother who, despite the bad reputation steel band had, was not opposing my interests in steel drums and encouraged me to pursue with my musical inclination but also believed that a further education was necessary to better myself in other domains and to give me more opportunities.

I left school at fifteen, the maximum age to end a government school and a free education as there were not so many choices for families who could not afford their children to go any further... Mywo, after having seen my recent dedication to study and my good results, did not want to deprive me of the opportunity to study some more and found an alternative by sending me to an Indian student for private lessons.

Only understanding years later the sacrifice she made in order to do this, I fully comprehended her reaction when she found out that I skipped the lessons...

When on my way to the student's house for my lesson, I would pass very close by the tree where I usually tuned pans and somehow I felt as if pulled in that direction. I would get side-tracked to that tree, never meaning to stay long but somehow time passed without being aware of it and realising too late that I had missed the lesson.

Why Mywo had not been informed about it, I can only guess that, as not to jeopardise his little side income, the student never mentioned it to her.

One afternoon under the tree, tuning pans with other boys, my mother was seen coming up the road, a friend warned me:

"Sterling look your Mum is coming up the road!"

I just dropped what I was doing and ran but Mywo had already seen me, without looking back, I heard her shouting, "Don't worry to run I 've seen you already you little vagabond, it's that am paying my money for? From now on no more private lessons if its pan you want I will buy pan for you instead"!

And she did. How wise and intelligent! Her attitude could be an example to many parents, but her approach in accepting my choice was not approved or well received by many of her friends and members of the family, they did not hide their disagreement nor criticism and many even opposed!

In front of all this adversity, Mywo would answer:

"Leave the child alone, you never know, one day it might take him to England!"

Mywo and her very special ways, always following her own instinct, despite the fact that all affiliation with steel bands was so dangerously considered.

Mywo never would have forced her own beliefs onto anyone, therefore always respected the choice of others without ever interfering between the person and the choice they had made.

That was 1946, five years later I would be chosen with twelve other steel band players to come to London for the Festival of Britain and tour England and France with the 'Trinidad All Steel Percussion Orchestra, T.A.S.P.O'.

T.A.S.P.O, was the first ever steel band to cross the ocean and the only music band from the colonies to play at the Festival of Britain."

Chapter VI
Tripoli

"In his spare time, Herman played with a band called Five Graves to Cairo after having mentioned me to Hugo Besson the captain, I was asked to tune their drums with Irwin Clement and Hugh Borde at their pan yard in Bellevue. I was also invited to tune for another band called Green Eyes from Woodbrook, that day I received five shillings, it was a lot of money to me.

Michael Natsy Constant was the leader of the band, his brother Bambi one of the players. Fifty years later, bumping into Bambi in Port of Spain, told me that after having seen me tune their pans in 1946, he got so inspired watching me that it influenced him to start tuning straight away, eventually becoming an excellent tuner.

We all had moved to Mywo's new boyfriend Horatio. He was a fisherman and we ate fish nearly every day and drank shark oil.

The house in which we had a room, stood at the corner of Ethell Street and Finland Street, it was rented from a 'bad john', Theodore Taylor, nicknamed 'Vatican. He was a shady character whose reputation for being 'all kind of things' and, most of all, terribly violent, preceded him, he was well known for cutting people with a razor that he always carried with him.

(Bad Johns always carried razors but if by any chance they happened to be without their weapons, they would say that they were naked).

I remember that in front of our house was a mango tree, its branches spreading wide over our roof and in the mango season some of the fruits would fall on the roof and when inside the house we heard the rolling of the fruits on the galvanized cover we would run outside shouting "mangoes," to catch the fruits before they hit the ground and get spoiled.

Tripoli, had their pan yard in Ethell Street, just around the corner from where we lived, giving me the opportunity to hang around the band more often, to play and tune their drums.

Herman was working at the American base, still dating his pretty wife to be, Elma Bynoe, while Sheila had moved to 14 Calcutta Street with her in-laws and Frank Mitchell the man she would later marry at sixteen.

In the meantime, while working at the American base and at the USO club, in Wrighthon Road, Herman recommended me for a job and for three months I worked on a construction site in Chaguaramas. The Batoo bus took about half hour to cover the eight miles between home and the base. One afternoon after work, as I was changing back into my clothes, I realised that my bus ticket was missing from my shirt pocket, I knew who the thief was but I, too afraid, did not dare confronting him for I knew he was a reputedly violent man much older and much bigger than me.

So I walked the eight miles home, where I was greeted with scorn and told off for being so late and careless. From then on my bus tickets were glued to my skin, eventually after three months I got fired for leaving too early.

I then worked at the Guardian, as a newspaper boy, a friend of my mother recommended me for the job; I would deliver the papers all over Port Of Spain on a bicycle from 5am to 8am and from 3 to 5pm for the evening news, the little I earned helped us at home and made me feel responsible to contribute to the household and helping Mywo who always worked hard.

Working from north to south and from west to east of POS, I would encounter the bands, whose pan yard were in those areas:

Invaders in Woodbrook, Casablanca in Belmont, constantly at war with each other. Casablanca would also fight Rising Sun whose base was also in Belmont, Tokyo from East Dry River would fight Invaders and so on... I, with Crossfire from the west and hitting all these areas during my newspaper rounds, made me very aware to keep a low profile and a neutral attitude towards the bands, the politics and fights, not getting involved in all the rivalry that went on between all, for fear of getting a beating...

The clashes with bands were notorious.

Herman was a lieutenant for the band 'Five Graves to Cairo', its captain, Hugo Besson, and one of the band's member, known as Brothers, were at war with two 'Bad Johns', Charles Samuel and 'Bad Man'. They would often be seen chasing one another with cutlass, as was the case that fateful night when, after a wild chase, Brothers, hiding by the gate of a churchyard, waited for Bad Man or Charles Samuel to turn up.

Bad Man looking for him all around, found himself standing right in front of the spot where Brothers was hiding. Startled by B jumping out of his hiding spot Bad Man legged it to the next street corner where Brothers caught up with him and hit him from behind with a cutlass blow on his shoulder. Staggering, Bad Man managed to get close to a house as he received the final blow cutting right from his shoulder into his torso.

The noise brought out a man from the house who, when looking down on Bad Man and seeing his shoulder hanging out from his body, assembled the hanging parts and gently put him on the pavement.

That night, when hearing the story, Herman quickly run home to burn his T-shirt with, Five Graves to Cairo, printed on it.

Bad Man died and that was the end of the band.

Brothers was finally caught and prosecuted despite all his mother's efforts to acquit him and the faith she had in Voodoo practice. For that purpose she had made the journey to Guyana to participate in a Voodoo ceremony and, as professed, turned up in court wearing a red dress and a red turban.

Brothers was hung.

1946 was the year for the first carnival to be allowed since the beginning of the war.

It was also around 1945/46 that bugles, were incorporated in steel bands, the buglers often were teenagers from the orphanage in Belle Eau Road, it gave them the opportunity to come out and join the bands at carnival. As many as eight buglers would be seen in one band, Casablanca, whose pan yard was in Argyle Street and close enough to the orphanage, had many. Red Army had an even bigger amount and was famous for its buglers.

Carnival Tuesday evening, as all the bands were parading down Charlotte Street, playing, walking with their steel drums around their necks, a fight broke out between Invaders from the west and Tokyo from the east.

Tokyo started the fight by throwing bottles and other missiles at Invaders, the latter fighting back, eventually had to retreat leaving their drums behind, some of which were taken by the Tokyo players.

(The next morning a twenty-five gallons drum named Barracuda was found hung on a lamppost).

When crossing Duke Street with Tripoli, we met the fight in full gear, getting caught up in the crowd trying to escape the ongoing turmoil, avoiding confrontation and running into the nearest houses, I turned the collar of my sailor jumper inside to hide the name of my band printed on it.

To be called a coward would not have entered my mind then, so afraid were we all of the violence we had witnessed and what ensued from it, I had made a purely instinctive decision to save my skin!

To give you an example of how fights would start with no reason at all and how bad guys would always seek any opportunity:

One afternoon going to meet Elma at a dance hall in Woodbrook, Herman, was stopped on his way by a gang of 'Bad Johns', one of them, 'Carlton', alias 'Black Head', wanted to know which area Herman came from:

"Partner where you from?"

"Hey Carlton…"

"You know me?"

"Yes, I live in Vatican yard!"

(The house we lived in belonged to a guy called 'Vatican' who lived in the house behind ours, it was nicknamed Vatican's yard).

Tripoli steel band knew that Vatican was known to all, to be a 'Bad John', famous for cutting people with razors or ferociously beat the life out of the object of his choice.

"Where you heading for?"

"To the dance in Woodbrook."

Another in the gang,, tapping a black jack in his hand said, "What's all this old talk we come to beat the fucking man let's get on with it."

My brother, with his slight and small frame, pretended to act cool contrarily to how he really felt inside, finally it was decided that they will give him some respite, slowly Herman walked away, trying to put in his gait, the nonchalant air that he was not at all feeling, he then heard Carlton's voice shouting behind him, "Wait, wait."

Herman froze and hesitated between running or keeping the same pace but thought better of it and stopped as he was definitely outnumbered.

Blackhead caught up with him. "Am going the same way to the dance."

Elma and her sisters, hearing the story from Herman who had arrived a couple of seconds before Blackhead and seeing, few minutes later, Blackhead walking through the door, just ran up to him holding him by the shirt, threatening him, "You see that man over there he is my man and wherever or whenever you see him you better leave him alone."

Through her father, Elma is related to the Manette family, in fact the famous and talented, Ellie Manette

(Invaders) is her cousin, known with his brothers, to be feared by all, it was no wonder why Blackhead's attitude towards Herman abruptly changed, also the fact that Elma and him went to the same school.

If men were scary, women were feared by most men as they would easily, by their fiery temper and shameless words, make one want to quickly disappear from their sight."

Elma is no timid person; her high spirited personality and quick witted repartees combined with an ingenuous disposition at relating her stories, arouse one's interest; when yesterday, I was listening to her singing voice relating a 'stick fight event' she had witnessed. I was taken by the laughter that accompanied every other sentence and find it impossible to translate on paper the atmosphere in which her voice had enchanted me, giving the story another dimension and transforming it into a memorable event:

When I was a teenager, my aunts took me to Toco, on the north coast for a week's vacation.

One evening there was a fete where I accompanied my aunts. There was a tent made of coconut branches and bamboos, where songs and dances were performed to the sound of drums, in the middle, a ring was formed, with all people standing around it, when we approached the front of the ring, to my horror, I saw blood all over the ring and on the two men standing there fighting with sticks, poking at each other's body, face and all! Being a teenager I was horrified seeing men wounding each other in this way, it was so violent, I could never forget it, I never saw that in Port of Spain so I believed it only happened in the country where people make their own entertainment as they have nothing better to do than watch people damaging each other!"

CARNIVAL a little history

It is nearly impossible to retrace with accuracy the origins of Carnival and when its birth took place, but in Trinidad, this custom was apparently brought by the French settlers in the 18th century, or by the African slaves brought onto the islands. Originally the European masquerades were held in the privacy of their homes, each individual wearing their own choice of costume, while the Africans would parade in the streets, a group of men wearing the same costume as a theme.

In France there is Mardis Gras, celebrated in February, it means 'Fat Tuesday', 'Shrove Tuesday', children know it as Pancake Day. In fact as a religious custom it is the last day to indulge in fatty food, maybe a custom that should be brought back into practice?

Mardis Gras was a celebration for the French planters and an old custom with masquerades, balls, costumes and masks, I have also read that its origins can be retraced to Italy, as a religious festival, it then spread to the Christian countries in Europe.

There was, before lent, a costume carnival with masks, beautiful dresses, wigs, music, 'Canboulay' (cannes brulees), sometimes, when the cane fields caught fire, the African slaves of the plantations estates were called to put out the fire, they marched to the fields carrying torches, while in their cars, the planters would be hurrying the slaves to overcome the fire to the sound of the horns.

At the emancipation of the slaves, J'Ouvert, (again a French word), ' jour ouvert' became the re-interpretation of Canboulay, parading the streets with lit torches to the sound of African drums.

In the early 19th century, workers were brought to the Caribbean, from central and west Africa, India and China as labourers, bringing with them their own traditions.

For example, the ancient African tradition of wearing masks and costumes and parading in villages often is associated with spirituality, a celebration for the dead or used as a healing power for the sick. Masks of feathers were worn for funeral ceremonies or harvest dances.

"As long as I can remember, the use of feathers in our costumes was a predominant feature in the Trinidadian carnival and it might have originated from the old African tradition of wearing feathers, who have one of the richest masks tradition in the world. In different cultures, feathers had different meanings and the thought that birds had spirit were represented in a wide range of themes, wisdom, courage…"

When slavery was abolished in 1838, the freed Africans were able to participate in the masquerades, soon enough the carnival was left to them, the beating of drums and their dances were not to be shared nor understood by the settlers, there had always been a separation between the two worlds. The natives couldn't never have enter the domain reserved to the settlers and the settlers lived away from the pulsing heart of the island, these passing colonials lived with a prejudice that had forbidden them from ever coming closer to the heart and soul of this large and unfortunate race, the heirs of an ancient world.

Most of the French left when the British colonials arrived.

We could say that the carnival was also used as a kind of rebellion against oppression, in a way it was a setting of disruption, as stick fighting and the steel band movement were at one point."

Chapter VII
Crossfire on an excursion to Rio Claro

"In Trinidad, fights were unfortunately a common occurrence, men with a fighting spirit would take any opportunity and sometimes no opportunity at all, just a glance could be enough to trigger their unrestrained and raging need for bloodshed, a need that always took over any common sense and there was no stop to their frustrated and fiery temper.

One morning, fifteen of us from Crossfire had taken our drums on an excursion to spend the day playing at Rio Claro, south east Trinidad.

We played during the train journey, entertaining all the passengers in our carriage. While we were taking a break, a voice rose from the back of the carriage urging us not to stop, it was Carlton, known as 'Black Head', offensive and dreaded for his constant need for a fight a really 'bad john' as we say in Trinidad...

Not giving him the benefit of our attention we carried on playing and stopping at random when it suited us, we knew too well to ignore his presence but when he became so persistently loud and obnoxious we all decided to stop playing altogether.

He suddenly got up, picked up two of our drums and threw them overboard, looking at us defiantly, brought a knife out of his pocket, snatched two more drums and before he could throw them, Imam's brother, Roger, (a bad john himself) stopped him by grabbing his arms while in the motion of swinging the drums through the open door. We just stood there looking at the knife and at the two of them holding and pulling at the drums, when finally they fiercely fought with one another, everyone around scattered, pushing each other and running away from the fight to other carriages.

While fighting, both coming closer to the door, Roger in a final struggle pushed Black Head out of the open carriage door, Black Head fell out of the speeding train onto the rail tracks, and we all screamed:

"Oh God, he dead."

Looking at Roger, we saw that his face was covered in blood and dripping onto his shirt but turning our attention there on the rail tracks where BH would have been lying, we saw him getting up brushing his clothes and walking away from the tracks.

Our excursion had taken an abrupt turn and while accompanying Roger to the hospital he went into an epileptic fit.

For this incident, Black Head was prosecuted and given a three months jail sentence, a place not so unfamiliar to him."

Chapter VIII
Operation Britain

In the mid-40s, due to the intense experimenting with the drums, pan tuners and players, were progressing fast in developing the steel bands.

This evolution had huge repercussion on the rivalry between the bands, riots in POS were numerous and a common occurrence.

"Some members of Casablanca went into the heart of Belmont which was 'Rising Sun' area, attacking anybody on their way, causing havoc and many injuries, which of course, brought the police in to captured some of Casablanca's offenders while others managed to disappear and hide far out in the countryside.

Eventually members of Casablanca, Invaders and Tokyo were taken to court for their constant fighting, pleaded guilty and finally discharged on the agreement not to engage in any more conflicts.

The fights between steel bands led the authorities to assume that they were a breeding ground for more trouble, violence and corruption, since the police interference did not produced much results in stopping the riots or even reducing the hostilities between the bands, a committee was formed in order to integrate steel bands within the society's structure and to consider it as a national art form.

Until then, the press had been condemning steel bands and its prodigious influence on people's attitude and thoughts needed to be shifted to a more positive and favourable aspect in regard to the steel band players.

The members of this committee would comprise respected men and few well connected with pans.

The steel band association was organised to protect from negative publicity, Trinidad's culture in the art form of steel band music, to give it respectability, extending it to reach at all different levels of the society and free expression.

The Honourable Albert Gomes, a great protector for the steel band men and music in general, inclined to any art form, gave the authorization to play in the streets from 6pm to 9pm when the ban was still on.

Sydney Gollop was the steel band association's first president, always fighting the cause of steel band men, often in court when a player was arrested. Later on he became a prominent figure in raising funds to send a steel band to Britain.(TASPO).

"One day riding his bicycle, Sydney Gollop bumped into Albert Gomes, a conversation ensued about his idea of sending a steel band to represent Trinidad at the Festival of Britain, an event occurring in London for the centenary of the 1851 Great Exhibition.

Few years ago, I met Gollop in Port of Spain who told me this story and how Albert Gomes was really the brainchild behind TASPO."

TASPO, Trinidad All Steel Percussion Orchestra was formed by the members of the association, twelve top pan musicians/tuners, were to be chosen from the leading steel bands of Trinidad, who were registered within the association.

'Operation Britain', as it was decided to name it, encountered many difficulties in fund raising, the government had declared that no financial assistance could be given to this project, the application having been made too late no funds were available, the association decided to raise themselves the necessary funding.

In April 1951, the Trinidad Guardian published an article:

The Trinidad and Tobago association has decided to make a community drive to secure funds necessary to tour England and to represent the Colony at the Festival of Britain...

The Mayor of Port of Spain launched an appeal for $7000 (Trinidad dollars) to be raised in order to send the steel band men to Britain, to this aim, a series of events were staged to raise money at which steel bands, Invaders, Tripoli, Crossfire, Chicago, City Syncopators, Kentuckians and Calypsonians performed.

Twelve drums were given by the Bermudez Biscuit factory, uniforms for the steel band players were offered to be made gratuitously by the owner of a tailoring firm.

Pan men went into the streets asking for donations, (sometimes pocketing the money for themselves) of course the Mayor and the Governor influenced the press to now write positive articles about the band and how this musical tour would reflects on tourism.

It was decided that the chosen musical director for TASPO would be Lieutenant Joseph Griffith, a talented musician born in Barbados, who played saxophone and clarinet in the Trinidad police band, he would also act as band leader.

"He played his saxophone and sang during the European tour.

The twelve pan men were then selected and I was one of them.

At the time of the election I was working at the Guardian newspaper when the list came on the radio:

Andrew de La Bastide (Chicago to Crusader)

Sterling Betancourt (Crossfire)

Belgrave Bonaparte (Southern Symphony

Philmore 'Boots' Davidson (City Syncopators)

Orman 'Patsy' Haynes (Casablanca)

Eliot 'Ellie' Mannette (Invaders)

Sonny Roach "Carlton" (Sun Valley)

Granville Sealey (Tripoli)

Dudley Smith (Rising Sun)

Winston Spree Simon (Fascinators)

Theodore Stephens 'Black James' (Free French)

Anthony Williams (North Stars)

Later on Granville Sealey was dropped, having asked money for himself and family, I suppose it was not well received as funds were already hard to raise.

My old school St Crispin, proud of their ex pupil's achievement in being chosen to represent Trinidad in Europe, organised a collection for a farewell present, they bought me a brown, sturdy, suitcase that I would carry with me for many years.

I never had a suitcase before so it represented a lot to me and really made me feel that I would travel!

I think our first main concert was at the Globe Theatre, the audience was ecstatic, for the first time orchestrated steel band music was heard, it also brought the public to believe in us and helped with raising more funds.

And we had become celebrities!"

The raising funds for 'Operation Britain, was no easy operation, it was obvious that the original sum of $7000 was not realistic so, for a few months it went on and on, trying to get private donors, functions were created for this reason, 'shilling jars' were placed in drugstores, halls were given for recitals, the financial situation was becoming crucial. Canon Farquhar, chairman of the finance sub-committee, published an article regarding the more profound aspect of Operation Britain and the positive repercussions it certainly would have on the steel band men and the cultural heritage of the colony.

Steel band players were considered by the majority as the underdog, generally despised by many and persecuted by the police forces, these boys often came from deprived background with not much of an education so it provided the players an opportunity for self-expression and a challenge that kept them totally immersed in.

O. B was in a way, an example for all the steel band men not to lose faith.

The Festival of Britain was to mark the centenary of the 1851 great industrial exhibition, TASPO, Trinidad All Steel Percussion Orchestra, led by Griffith, had to be well rehearsed and the new pans acquired were all made from the large fifty gallons oil drums.

"Ellie Mannette made three bass drums and Anthony Williams two pairs of tenor boom (cellos) one pair for Dudley Smith and one for himself, it was an innovation in steel band. Anthony Williams also made the fourth and fifth tenor pan which is now the standard pattern most steel band players use.

All these new changes made a huge difference to the sound of the drums and to our playing. All the players were able to tune their own instrument with the exception of Patsy Haynes whose pan was made by Boots Davidson.

The press, in general was quite supportive of Operation. Britain, greatly influencing people's minds.

Griffith also improved our knowledge of music, until now most of us never had read a musical partition so with the actual numbers notes were written, the steel drum is a chromatically pitched percussion instrument, a drum carries the full chromatic range of notes.

So in Griffith's arrangements full chords were utilised, our repertoire went from classical tunes to calypso to marches, his aim was to demonstrate the adaptability of the steel drum and the many different variations it can produce.

Griffith was a disciplinarian and had to be with all of us, talented maybe, but never having rehearsed so intensely before; we were learning many new tunes and these practices were showing our potential as musicians, it also made us feel good and professional. Our rehearsal headquarters was in a youth centre in Cocorite, the rehearsals went on for about three months.

After the departure date had been postponed due to bad weather we finally, on the 6th July, arrived at the docks, the ovation of thousands of supporters who had come to wish us well was an emotional moment for all the families and relatives who had come to see 'their boys' off. The press was also there taking pictures and when a journalist asked Philmore 'Boots, Davidson what he will be doing in England, 'Boots' replied with great assurance that he will teach the King how to beat pan!

Invaders played their version of the song:

My heart cries for you
Sighs for you
Dies for you
My heart cries for you
Please come back home.

It brought many tears to people's eyes, Mywo was there and so were Herman and Sheila and so with sadness, joy and anticipation we left the island of Trinidad to an unknown world."

From the day you all heard your names coming up to be part of TASPO and the involvement that followed with the numerous rehearsals where you had to give the best of yourselves to the euphoria your performances created, you all must have been on a high, far from grasping the reality of your departure.

How did you feel when it all dawned on you that you were actually leaving all without having the faintest idea of what lied ahead?

"I personally felt good, I was playing and going to a country to represent my island,

It was an important event in the history of Trinidad being the only colony to send an orchestra to the Festival of Britain, we often heard about Britain, it felt as it was just a distant place where existed a real king and queen!

Only later did I feel a kind of nostalgia and sadness in missing my folks.

We left on the banana boat, the *San Mateo*, in July 1951.

We made two stops, in Martinique and in Guadeloupe to pick up a load of bananas and students travelling to France, there we gave radio shows and concerts organised for us in Fort de France where we remained for a few days.

While on the islands, some of the boys had already lost their heads at the sight of the pretty Martiniquais, in return they received unexpected ailments and I saw Griffith, his hands on his head with despair, an attitude of his that I would often witness; we were only at the beginning of our journey and he seemed to anticipate the worse!

The hotel we stayed at in Fort de France was one of the many where prostitutes took their clients, the rooms had bidets, none of us had seen a bidet before, inevitably someone without giving it a second thought and mistaking it for the loo caused havoc, the blockage provoked a flood all over the room to finally leak into the restaurant down below.

Griffith, his hands on his head again, looking up in vain!

I can easily imagine the thoughts that went through his head at the time!

We also had to leave Sonny Roach behind in Martinique after being diagnosed with tonsillitis.

Duddley Smith, one of our tenor bass players was also the band's barber, he kept his razor in a red box with on it, written in gold, the name 'Photo'.

Over one of his trimming session, not sure what had caused his anger I suddenly saw his razor slashing the air:

"Anybody interfering with me ith photho in their backside." (Failing, due to his pre-eminent lisping, to make the dramatic impact hoped for).

"Duddley why don't you shut your ass"? replied Boots.

"Well they thaid my uncle was not going to shoot anybody? Well apparently he shot a woman didn't he ?"

None of it was to be taken too seriously; it was a lot of talk just to impress the others!

You cannot imagine how silly and juvenile some of us were, this kind of talk could also have been to reassure and boost their manhood or so they thought!

But that red box with the gold letters 'Photo' written on it had made quite an impact on me as I up to now remember!

During the long journey to France, we played music and the many students who were travelling with us performed in plays, we entertained each other and we shared many laughs and games, there were happy moments, forgetting a little bit all we had left behind. But the words Mayo whispered with tears in her eyes when bidding me farewell at the docks would ring in my head:

"This is your opportunity son, don't worry about us, you 'd be a fool to come back !"

And in a more colourful way, my brother's words,
"You'd be a damn ass if you come back!"
These few words will forever be stored in my mind.
When in doubt I will bring them back to the surface for comfort and to remind me not to give up."

Chapter IX
Bordeaux/ London/Paris

"By a sunny and warm July morning, we finally docked at Bordeaux.

At the wharf, playing on deck, people soon gathered around the ship and faces were seen at the windows of the nearby buildings, we could see them looking at us through binoculars.

To these country folks, we must have been such a foreign sight, beating on these old rusty drums!

We left Bordeaux late that evening on the overnight train to Paris.

It was our first time on a sleeper and lying on the top of a bunk bed, rocked to the rhythm of the wheels on the rail tracks, I thought of hearing a Tamboo Bamboo band playing and I just lay there wide awake, transported so very far away from all reality.

On our arrival in Paris the next morning we were horrified at seeing the porters throwing our drums out of the luggage compartment onto the platform as if they were dustbins, they were really startled when told that these bins were actually musical instruments which we were to tour England with, they quickly apologised.

After having changed stations and waiting at the Gar du Nord for the Paris-London boat train, we sat at the empty chairs and tables placed in the open station and 'limed'....(a Trinidadian expression describing a get together).

While we all chatted, a waiter came waving his hand in the air as if he was chasing flies,

" Allez, Allez", said he. If we did not understand the words, we got the message from his waving hand and were bewildered to be hushed away from the chairs in this manner. We certainly were not familiar with the existence of cafes inside stations and candidly thought, that these chairs and tables had been placed there for anyone's use.

Remaining in the train at Calais, the sleeping cars were loaded aboard a ship and sailed across the Channel.

We were told that the Golden Arrow train hauled by a steam engine had few more Pullman cars added to coincide with the Festival of Britain exhibition in London.

On arrival at Victoria Station, we were met by the Trinidadian, Edric Connor, who drove us to his basement flat, on Bayswater Road.

All through the drive, I kept looking out of the window, wondering how one could ever find his way through the vastness of this city and while passing 'Speakers Corner" in Hyde Park, Edric explained to us that it was a spot where people expressed their opinion on various subjects, most often to do with politics or religion, same way as we back home communicate through our Calypso songs.

We were all to share rooms at the King's Court Hotel in Leinster's Terrace, mine was to be shared with Duddley Smith.

Edric Connor was a baritone and a famous calypso singer who gave lectures on West Indian folksongs and dances. He was a well-known Shakespearian actor also for his role in 'Moby Dick' starring Gregory Peck.

He was in charge of us in London. I had never previously met Edric in Trinidad but had heard of him and how, when the American naval base had been established in Trinidad pushing people out of their dwellings, he had helped the families to be re-accommodated. At the time I met him in London he must have been in his late 30s and had been living there for a few years.

We rehearsed at Edric's and would walk the short distance from our hotel to his flat, so afraid were we of losing ourselves in this limitless city. In our spare time we would only venture as far as the 'Speaker's Corner' in Marble Arch, listening to the speeches or debates that were going on there, learning that many famous politicians spoke there, like Karl Marx and Lenin, the journalist and author George Orwell... At dusk, we also noticed the many prostitutes standing by the trees and lying on the grass having sex there and then, making their living the only way they knew how.

The day came, when we were to make our appearance at South Bank, outside Festival Hall for the innovative Festival of Britain.

The Festival introduced new styles in architecture, furnishing, fashion, fabrics, new materials, like fibreglass, plywood, plastics...

Our yellow coach, with Trinidad All Steel Percussion Orchestra written in large letters on both sides, left us by the Westminster entrance; people were everywhere, walking to all the different parts of the exhibition, stopping and looking curiously as our drums were loaded onto trolleys and at us dressed in colourful tropical shirts and Stetson hats. Feeling that we must be one of the curiosities at the South Bank exhibition they escorted us to our performing spot.

Setting up our drums, a crowd of people had formed around us laughing and chatting while staring at the rusty drums, through the first tune we could hear people's comments like; "It must be black magic" and started to dance to our music.

We received a great ovation.

Few famous Trinidadians were amongst the crowd to give us their encouragement and support, beside Edric, was the 100 meters Olympic runner McDonald Bailey, P.L. Ulric Cross, a famous pilot during World War II and many musicians who were puzzled at this extraordinary instrument arriving from Trinidad

We gave a concert at the St Pancras Town Hall on the 2nd August, with the Calypsonians, Roaring Lion and Lord Kitchener, the baritone, Edric Connor, and Boscoe Holder's dance troupe. We performed at the Savoy Hotel, which at the time showed the best cabaret acts and at the Royal Albert Hall.

During a performance at the Lyceum we were amused and refrained from giggling when, to our Calypso music, a few people danced the foxtrot.

T.A.S.P.O was well received and we were given enthusiastic review in all the newspapers.

We made our first television appearance for a half hour BBC show ;Caribbean Cabaret; with Edric Connor, Boscoe

Holder's dance company and Lord Kitchener. Hundreds of people who had seen the show where telephoning to congratulate the BBC before the show even ended, it was such a success that the BBC spoke of repeating the entire show at the annual Radio Show to give the public a chance to see the best of broadcasted radio and television programmes. It was said that within this small studio at Alexandra Palace, we recreated some of the Trinidad carnival atmosphere, the backdrop had been created with bamboos, on the other side a beach scene for the dancers."

The Roaring Lion, was in fact the stage name for Rafael de Leon, a famous calypso singer and composer, who could write on many different themes, sometimes with very explicit lyrics. Some of his songs were banned for a while, but he was then, one of the very few Calypsonians who could read and write musical notation!

In the 1930s he recorded in New York and probably the first Calypsonian to record abroad with his friend ,Attila the Hun'.

He matched his powerful stage name by always carrying with him a lion headed cane and presented himself always impeccably dressed.

He certainly was known for his linguistic prowess.

In the mid-90s, Eddy Grant recorded one of his songs: 'Papa Chunks'.

"Boscoe and his wife, Sheila Davies Clarke, had a dance group, Boscoe, was a dancer a painter and a very good pianist, he and Sheila were the first to bring two steel drums to London with their dance troupe and both playing the instruments.

I have few funny stories concerning Boscoe, as with many other Trinidadians in London, we evolved more or less, in the same crowd. A couple of years after my arrival in London, Boscoe asked to paint my portrait, we all knew about his homosexuality despite the fact that he was married to Sheila the dancer.

The few times I met him he always came up with the same request of wanting to paint my portrait. I was unsure as to accept. It was Russel whom I had already met and shared a flat with who pushed me to have my portrait done: "Come on you are a big boy of twenty-three, what are you afraid of?" said he on one occasion.

I was very shy and I suppose a bit naive for my age believing all sort of rumours about homosexuality and how in Trinidad they were chased and beaten after having been set up. A man there had to be macho to be respected.

Anyway I arrived in Holloway, where Boscoe and his wife lived and after the usual greetings, Sheila went out.

Boscoe asked me to sit on the stool he had placed in the middle of the room for that purpose, then started to paint, only to stop some time later to ask me to remove my shirt, for he wanted a cleaner line, which I did and kept posing in my white vest. A while later I was asked again to remove my vest: "No no no Boscoe if you want to paint me it will have to be just so!"

He carried on painting.

Eventually when years later, Boscoe moved to Trinidad he took all his art work with him. Few years ago, when running into him in Port of Spain, I asked him about the portrait, "That's gone" he replied and proposed to paint another one but never came around to do it, he died three years later.

In retrospective I regret for not having taken the time to fulfil his request.

His work is justly recognised, he was an artist in every sense of the word.

If the same situation had taken place years later, even as shy and candid as I was, it would not have left such an impression on me.

Again in 1964 when every Sunday night, Russel and I were playing at the Rockingham Club in Archer Street, members only and famously known to the gay community, Boscoe, as usual turned up at the club inviting us to a party he was going to in Hampstead later on that evening. Russel, I and two other friends, too happy at the thoughts of meeting girls arrived at the house in Hampstead.

At the door we were led to a dimly lit room, we could barely make out who were the people dancing. The only existing light from the ceiling gave a red glow and seemed masked with a cloth, finally spotting a couch, the four of us sat waiting for our eyes to get used to the red smoky haze, when our gazes finally swept the room we could see that the crowd consisted only of men dancing together or standing talking, drinking.

Looking at each other, the four of us exchanged meaning glances to depart when Boscoe appeared dancing towards us, leading his partner and shouted to us in a reproaching tone: "Why you all don't get up and swing?"

And we did.

Russ and I got up holding each other and danced to the front door, our two friends following us. We were all in stitches, laughing all the way to the car for having been deceived so cunningly.

To tell the story is not half as funny as it was in real, you can imagine us all, with whatever our anticipation or expectations were of meeting girls!

I have to speak about Chris Lemaitre, a man who contributed to my staying in London and helped many others. (Chris died in 2012).

After one of our performances at Kings Cross Town Hall, Chris, a slight and little man, came to congratulate us saying that he never thought that a steel band could sound so sweet; he recalled to us when in the early 40s while walking in the streets of Port of Spain, heard in the distance a strange sound that led him to a group of men beating some tins with the same continuous and monotonous tone: pelelepong pelelepong. That evening, Chris expressed his thrill at the musical arrangement, the variety of the tunes and the sweet sound of our drums, astonished was he at the improvement steel band had made.

Late that evening, all sitting with Chris, he advised us to come back to London after our trip to Paris, that he will look after us and would try to organise gigs. Five of us agreed.

Chris had successfully passed his law degrees in London, he was already a fervent communist and had joined the party. I always have had a great admiration for his integrity, he totally lived according to his beliefs, with an acute intelligence and a very sharp sense of humour, his knowledge covered many fields and you could sit and listen to him for hours, he was definitely a born orator. I have not met many men like him and still at 90 his wit is was sharp and caustic as ever.

Our last London performance before touring the UK was for a BBC television show in Alexandra Palace, after which, we were all off giving concerts in many cities in England, Wales and Scotland, travelling in our coach with 'Trinidad All Steel Percussion Orchestra' written on each side. We also had contracts to play at all the Mecca dance halls in the whole of Great Britain.

Everywhere, our music was always received with enthusiasm. it had been a very successful journey.

In between the tour we would come back to London for a few days.

When Griffith was suspected to withhold money from us, one night, a couple of 'Bad Johns', Simon Spree and Boots, went to Griffith bedroom door, shouting abuses, of him being a crook and a thief and urging him to come out to face them and talk; they were of course under the influence of alcohol to pluck up the courage they did not have during the day to confront him.

They eventually got hold of empty bottles, throwing and smashing them against his door. Griffith never came out, neither anyone else did.

The next day, not to be thrown out by the hotel manager, we had to make up a story."

It is during these London breaks that Sterling would meet his first girlfriend, Mary. Knowing his succinct answers when I question him on feelings and emotions and in order not to meet his impatience and reticence, I was cautious in approaching his encounter with Mary. Going over it few times, Sterling probably said as much as I could hope for.

"I knew you would ask!

One evening we all went to a student dance in Hans Crescent, Knightsbridge, Duddley Smith who, while in London had met a girl he knew from Trinidad, Sybille Batson, came to the dance with her and an Irish friend of hers, Mary.

Both were working as nurses. After having spent most of the evening walking about and looking at the dancers, I plucked up some courage and invited Mary for the last dance.

As a friend of Duddley it felt a bit less scary and a little more comfortable, I was also aware of her glancing in my direction.

My usual inhibition added to my inexperience with women, made me quite insecure.

In Martinique when most of the boys were running amok with the local girls, Anthony Williams and myself kept very quiet and received the nickname of 'cave men' to which we used to reply that we wanted to save ourselves for Europe.

Mary and I just danced and parted after the ball. A week later, Duddley and I met the two friends at Lancaster Gate station, walking on Bayswater Road towards our hotel, I really felt embarrassed when Mary took hold of my arm. I did not know how to free myself without hurting her feelings, so I remained hooked, constantly aware of being stared at by the passers-by. In Port of Spain I never had much contact with the white folks there, there was a distinctive separation in the places familiar and approachable to my class, therefore my unease at walking arm in arm with Mary in broad daylight.

In the hotel lobby we met the boys playing table tennis, of course we were greeted with the usual jokes and laughter. Only later did I take Mary to my room.

Chris certainly played an important role in my return to London, five of us had decided to listen to Chris's advice and come back to London after Paris, Edric had offered to keep the bulk of our belongings until our return.

In Paris we were to play for two weeks at the Medrano Circus, and recorded under the 'Vogue' label."

MEDRANO CIRCUS
PARIS OCT 19TH 1951

The circus dated back from 1897, Jerome Medrano, the son and famous clown Boum Boum, when old enough, took up the running of his father's circus in Paris Montmartre, in 1928.

Many great artists were to perform there, singers, acrobats, dancers, the famous French singer, Charles Trenet also performed at the circus.

"There was a rider, Michele Marconi, dressed in red, dancing next to her white horse with her legs all in black in total synchrony with the horse's feet, she had those dancers shoes like the ballerinas…there was an act with two acrobats, also six cyclists who at the end of their act made a pyramid with just one on the bicycle and, one after the other they jumped on the predecessor's shoulders with the dramatic rolling of the drums until the last one has made it to the top of the pyramid, then the men who formed it jumped back on the ground as the rolling of the drums grows fainter and fainter.

There was a real circus atmosphere then, with the smells, the sawdust on the ground of the arena...there was a cavalry and a black ice skater on a small podium, performing amazing and prodigious figures on this tiny socle, he was named Count Leroy. There were the clowns, Pipo and Beby, with their famous double act...we did not know really what it was all about not speaking French, except that just by looking at their body language and their mimics it was funny, there was a continuous laughter from the audience.

We played for a couple of weeks at the circus. Jerome Medrano had made a big introduction for TASPO, a steel band in France was also a novelty. There was always a moment of silence when we came into the arena with our instruments, then after hearing the first few notes, the atmosphere changed and the audience would give us a great ovation, people clapped and clapped...We loved it!

On our spare time we visited Paris, dazzled by all the sights and the city lights, we foolishly spent all our pennies. Griffith, not wanting any of us to go back to England, for he knew that five of us had left some of our things behind in the intention to go back there, was distributing our money very sparingly. Sadly in the end we had to send for the suitcases and forget about our returning to England.

Some members were becoming restless, a fight broke out between Belgrave Bonaparte and Boots who got stabbed and had to be hospitalised and Griffith, his hands on his head cursing all the French gods..

In Port of Spain I had seen many clashes and fights, always avoiding that sort of environment, after what I saw that day in Paris I made up my mind not to return to Trinidad and get back to London at all costs! The words my brother had whispered in my ear when I left Port of Spain echoed in my head:

"You'd be a dammed ass if you come back."

I had Mary's address so I sent her a telegram asking if she could advance the train fare for the five of us, she generously forwarded £10, enough to take us all back.

I do not know if it was the cold weather and the prospect of having to face the coming winter that had dampened some of the members' determination to remain in Europe or the warning of our great calypsonian, Lord Kitchener:'

"There is no bad John in England the only bad John is the cold."

Of course we were all home sick but I alone remained.

Griffith was reluctant in handing me back my passport promising me that TASPO will come back next year, that he already had contracts for us but I had made up my mind and when that evening Griffith and I sat at the hotel bar, it dawned on him that I will not be shaken in my decision. Finally he gave me his blessing remarking that I was a brave boy.

I was twenty-one.

The following day at the Paris station, they all bade me farewell, Duddley telling me how I will suffer from the cold, Philmore, with his arms in a sling, wished me luck, all in their own ways. I had tears in my eyes, which I was trying to suppress, it was such a sad moment for all of us, each with his own personal doubts.

After all we had spent four months together, I felt very alone and facing them leaving I had doubts about the decision I had made to stay."

Chapter X
London is the Place for Me
1951/55

"During the long boat train journey to England, alone for the first time since weeks, I had time to reflect on my situation and suddenly felt the doubts, fear and insecurity that my decision in remaining in London generated. I was beginning to experience what it felt like to be completely alone in a foreign country and suddenly grasping at the amplitude of my decision, I was scared.

Wondering if I was demented to come back to this foreign country with the only fragile link being a woman I hardly knew, for whom my feelings were ambiguous!

Looking through the cold window at the speedy landscape did not help the state of mind I was in, all I could see was a pretty dim sight as the fog had settled over the French countryside.

I had been warned that winters in England were far worse.

Few sailors passing by my compartment seeing the steel drum, took this opportunity to engage in a conversation, they were friendly and wanted to know where I was going and so on. I found myself saying that I was on my way to London to meet the other musicians. My spontaneous answer made me feel even worse, maybe I was just trying to reassure myself that I wasn't so alone and dissipate the uneasy mood I had been in since I had left the others.

At Victoria Station, a sudden rush of ease and warmth took over all my being and the disquiet state of mind I had been in for most part of the journey improved when, at my arrival on the platform, I saw, Chris Lemaitre, Sybille, Mary and a couple who I was to meet for the first time: Noris Straker and his girlfriend. I, then experienced a complete release of all my fears, this reunion brought back all the confidence that kept eluding me during the journey and provided a re-comforting sensation.

Norris drove us to his home in Gloucester Road to a Caribbean dinner he had cooked for us, and when the welcoming party left, prepared a mattress on the floor for me to stay the night, all around me was generosity and protection I was so grateful for.

Chris, the following day, met me at Norris and took me to a friend of his, a landlady who rented rooms for students in Castelton Road, Barons Court, graciously, Chris, took care of the rent deposit, we then walked to the labour exchange in Hammersmith in order for me to sign on and receive my ration book for the landlady to provide me with two meals a day.

I was soon to find out how the softly spoken Chris gave so much thought and time in helping others and how his generosity did not only extend to provide but to really care for his country fellows.

A month later I was sent by the labour exchange, to work in a lumber yard in Putney, braving the snowy December morning I turned up on the job not really equipped for the cold weather, when in the yard, I saw a bunch of men wearing scarves wrapped around their heads and necks, hands in gloves moving the snow covered planks of wood, I just stood there bare hands in my borrowed RAF coat, and finally walked away.

I notified the employment agency that the vacancy had already been taken. I had not yet grasped the difficulty at finding a job.

When Chris gave a Christmas party at his flat in Earls Court, I brought my steel drum and played well into the evening, some accompanied me by singing and drumming with their hands on the table, or on anything they could bring rhythm out of. When, at the end of the evening we all had to catch the last tube, Chris who had been shaking the maracas, decided to walk down the street with us and play on the way to the tube station, so jolly were we that we did not even stopped at the sight of a policeman standing at the underground entrance. He just looked at us smiling and greeted us with a " Merry Christmas."

Most of Chris's friends were academics or intellectuals from Trinidad and like him studying at university with the ambition to perfect themselves to higher degrees of qualification, it was evident that Chris would eventually encourage me in receiving further education.

He spoke of a Polytechnic in Regents Street where I should enrol. He had seen me spending time making a steel drum out of dustbins, failing, as the galvanised material was not responding very well. I had shared with him the idea of forming a group with some of his friends who in their spare time, were all for it. I finally had to give up the idea.

Mary lived in the nurse's home in East Ham and would spend her day off with me in London, often returning home on the last evening train.

One evening, missing her train, Mary came back to the house, waking up the landlady to open the front door when, both smelled gas coming from my room, shaking me awake they switched off the gas fire that I had failed to turn off adequately.

Mary's patience with me not working, was gradually evaporating, the little money I had was entirely spent and I had not yet repaid my debt of the £10 she had so kindly lent me for the train fare back to London. Our relationship soon came to an end.

I was also pretty demoralised at not getting any work with my steel drum, or for that matter at this stage, any job would have lifted my spirits.

It was certainly not as easy as I thought to earn a living as a steel drum musician. Only then did I realise how safe and protected I had been while with TASPO, how with the group I only had to concentrate on my playing and nothing else. In the summer London had appeared cheerful and full of opportunities with all the concerts we gave there and all over Britain and now I had landed into a depressing and harsh reality.

Funny enough, the day following my break up with Mary, I got a full time job at the Lyons ice cream factory in Olympia.

After my first wage pack I moved to Gunterstone Road in Barons Court where two of Chris's friend lived: Norris Straker and Harriet. I rented a room on the second floor.

For the first time since my arrival in London I had to shop and cook for myself and ended eating a lot of baked beans on toast, unaware of the existence of the 1950 fish fingers invention!! Later on I practised cooking remembering the taste of my mother's recipes, using tins of corn beef or salmon.

I worked in the ice cream factory for few months. There, with many others, I was in a line wearing gloves and a gown putting ice cream in the packing machine which at the end of the day we sterilized. In September I was offered a permanent job in the steak and kidney pie department, of course I accepted, Norris was already working there placing pies on trays and into a huge oven, this was our routine through the day and when my eyes got so inflamed from the transition of heat from the oven and the cold from outside and had to receive a series of injections at Moorfield Hospital, I knew that my days in this job will soon come to an end.

That end came a couple of months later when I got fired after having had a disagreement with the foreman, it was just a question of perspective on who was right or wrong and he was in a powerful position.

I remember the freezing winter of 1952 and the December great smog apparently due to heavy coal combustion producing so much sulphur dioxide that the air was saturated with it and you could taste its acridity.

Fog was not unusual in London, but this was unseen before and for five days brought the whole city to a standstill, and any form of transport. You could not see one metre in front of you, it finally dispersed with the winds.

Once driving in Hyde Park with Russel, not finding the right exit we drove around and around for I do not know how many times! Other cars were following us not knowing where to exit either!

At another student dance, I met Moira, an Irish singer, her brother P J. Scott was then, a famous saxophonist and arranger, the relationship lasted a couple of years, for both it had not been a passionate love story.

In 1953 Chris mentioned that a musician from Trinidad was in London and that the two of us should meet.

Russel Henderson was then studying piano tuning in Kentish Town where he lived, he already worked in a couple of West End clubs, our musical relationship was to last for many years, he also became one of my closest friends.

I suddenly felt protected with Russel, not only the fact that he was six years older than me but that he, while practising piano, earned a living with it while I was still looking for a break as a steel pan musician.

Russel also had contacts with record companies as a session musician.

With him I felt I was at last entering, for the first time since in London, the world of music I had so longed for.

Apart from having the same musical inclination and the fact we were both totally hopeless at securing our future, we had very contrasting personalities and naturally different needs, but for both the future was so far away! In the school where Russ was studying piano tuning, my steel drum generated much interest having never encountered such an instrument before, it was tested on a machine that could not provide any proper reading for it. They were puzzled by the sound and at the notes.

Knowing some of the recording studios for having had sessions with calypsonians, Russel thought of making a record together, for this he composed 'Ping Pong Samba' and 'Ping Pong Lullaby', with him on piano, Fitzroy Coleman on guitar, Neville Buckarut on bass, Carl Francis on drums and I on my ping pong steel drum.

The 45 record was eventually released with Melodisc and sent to Trinidad to be played on the radio every morning.

In the course of our partnership, Russel and I made many more records, the last one in 1966 'West Indian Nights'.

Living at the opposite end of London, Russel in Kentish Town and I in Barons Court, we decided to move together and shared a flat in Cromwell Road.

Every night, Russ, played the piano in a clip joint on Gerard Street, I would come in the evening to meet him and watch the other musicians, specially the drummer, looking and listening to the music every night feeling frustrated in not playing, with the only consolation was that I had come closer to music, even if steel band was not yet considered. I quickly realised that if it was easier to find a job as a drummer, I could easily learn to play and shared my determination with Russel who thought that in order to be a really good drummer it was a rather formidable task to take on. He eventually changed his mind when, one evening the drummer offered me his seat to experiment with his drums and was told that I had the skills required to play such an instrument.

Soon after I met a famous jazz drummer, Tony Kinsey, who played also at the Flamingo Club with Ronnie Scott, a baritone saxophonist, Tony gave me a dozen lessons and taught me how to roll."

After having mourned their King, in the summer of 1953, England was looking at the biggest broadcasting event of the decade, the coronation of Queen Elizabeth the Second, there were many street parties, hundreds of thousands of spectators poured in the capital, many were seen camping out along the coronation route, to gradually be joined by millions from across the nation and the world!

There were fireworks over the Embankment, London was really celebrating their Queen.

"Of course we were part of the spectators in Regents Street, I remember the Queen of Tonga waving in an open carriage under the pouring rain receiving an enormous ovation.

Just before Christmas 1953, a circus was auditioning musicians for their show, having previously played with TASPO at the Medrano Circus in Paris, I held all hopes and was naively confident that my steel drum would definitely be of interest. Russel came with me in case they also needed a pianist. After playing a couple of tunes I was told that it was too much of a risk to take on an act with such a weird instrument. I was totally distraught and walking back to our flat on the Cromwell Road, holding in my hand the cold metal pan that felt like ice, my hopes of performing as a steel band musician deserted me. On the bridge, crossing the railway line at West Cromwell Road, I raised my drum to hurl it over the parapet wall when Russel's hand grabbed my arm in time to prevent me from doing so, took the drum from me and carried it safely back to the flat. It was during this walk that for the first time we spoke about having a steel band together, the only major problem was how to acquire drums, London was hardly the place to find them and to make such instruments.

Some weeks before, my brother had written from Port of Spain, announcing that an old school friend of mine, Mervyn Constantine, was thinking of coming to London and if I could eventually meet him and put him up for a while. I wrote back asking Herman if Anthony Williams, who had also come up with TASPO and now was captain and tuner for the North Star Steel Band, (the band my brother was with), could make a couple of drums for us, a guitar pan (nine notes) and a second pan (thirteen notes) and that Mervyn could bring them with him on his trip to England.

Which he did a couple of months later.

Mervyn moved in with us, he was not a musician but we desperately needed a third player to form our steel band, and he was the only person around, so I taught him to play. With Russel it was different, having been around the pan men back home and being already a pianist it was easier for him.

We rehearsed in our room day after day, my evenings were spent in the West End where Russ played, waiting for him to finish we would then walk and pop in the other clubs around.

The basement at the Sunset Club, in Carnaby Street was very much a 'black meeting place' a very popular venue for famous jazz musicians, the jazz cognoscenti; the alto saxophonist Joe Harriet, Ronnie Scott, Billy Ekstine and many others. Shirley Bassey who had just arrived from Cardiff, sang there and at the Taboo Club in Greek Street. During these evening anyone who played an instrument would join the actual band on the small stage for a session, people were 'doing turns' and in the course of the night many musicians would have exchanged places.

The people who intermingled in these clubs formed a crowd of American service men with girls, prostitutes, pimps who had girls on the streets and of course we would meet with some of the characters. There was this incredible atmosphere taking you away from all existing form of reality, it created a world without barrier, a world of free expression where everyone mixed, famous with non-famous, stars and gangsters, pimps with high society, Ava Gardner, Peter Sellers and Princess Margaret to name a few...I assume that the fact of brushing slightly with the underworld 'the dangerous classes' flavoured with glamour, provoked in some people an attractive challenge.

Of course the music was really the link in this demi-monde environment!

Club owners had girls for sale attracting high profile men who would send for them, clubs were often linked to organised crime like pimping and the owners of such clubs were usually kept in check by the authorities.

At the Sunset Club, we would often hear of a party where we would all go, not always knowing who gave it, never returning home before 5am, for instance we would go to Chelsea to a party organised for Sammy Davies Junior and his wife Brit Eckland, never having met them before.

Our calypsonian, Lord Kitchener performed at the Sunset, he often amused himself by provoking the police. Leaving the club in the early hours of the morning with few of us, walking down Regent street, Kitchener, sighting two policemen coming in the opposite direction towards us, told us to have a good look at what would follow and with this, he turned around and started to run, jacket flapping in the wind. The two policemen who were about to pass us started to run after him, Kitchener then, abruptly stopped, turned around to face the two men and greeting them with a puzzled look on his face:

"What are you running for?" said one of the policemen.

"Is there a law that says a man cannot run in the morning officer?"

The men confused at what to say or do and glancing in our direction, decided that it was probably better to leave this mad man alone.

The Sunday evenings at the Sunset Club were dedicated to a cabaret consisting of many different acts. We informed Mr Leslie, the Jamaican manager of the club that we had formed a steel band, not ever having heard of this instrument before, agreed to have us on a trial the following Sunday, just to suss out the audience's reaction.

In the meantime we had decided to call it 'The Russ Henderson Steel Band Trio'.

That evening the reaction of the spectators was so enthusiastic that we got hired to play every Sunday.

At last there was light at the end of the tunnel!

We were then approached by Paul Clinton, a musical agent who booked us for a resident gig at one of the night club ' La Ronde', off Piccadilly in Swallow Street, next to 'The Stork Club'.

We got together with musicians we knew; on double bass and bass pan, Max Cherrie, on the accordion Conrad Martinez from Ceylon, Giggi Walker on the trumpet, Russel on piano and second pan, I on the drums and tenor pan. We would play as a conventional band and in the course of the performance, three of us, Russ, Max and I, would switch to play the steel drums.

Max, eventually became the first pianist to play the bass pan and shaking the maracas at the same time, which later on became popular amongst steel band players.

One evening after living La Ronde, chatting and walking down Regent Street heading towards the Sunset Club, Russel, with a girl on his arm, abruptly stopped, looking just ahead of him as his current girlfriend appeared a few meters away heading in our direction. Russel was so fast at turning back and disappearing across the road, that only the two girls were left to face each other.

Girls flaunted themselves at the noticeably handsome Russel who often had to run away to avoid his own confusion!

There was no nastiness in our behaviour, we were just enjoying the superficialities that life could offer, living in the present, totally irresponsible of any consequences or repercussions that our carefree attitude could achieve, relationships came and went without us giving it a second glance.

There was certainly no discrimination and we accepted with a very relaxed attitude whatever or whoever came our way.

During the club runs most faces had become familiar we all lived entirely excluded from everyday reality.

My old school friend, Irwin, arrived from Trinidad, leaving behind 'The Original Limbo Dancers' company, who he was playing Congo drums with and who were to finish filming in the London studios their appearance in the film, 'Fire Down Below', shot in Trinidad and starring Robert Mitchum. Finally, tired of waiting for the group's departure, Irwin decided to make his own way to London.

Asking around for me, Irwin was taken by a friend of his to La Ronde night club where we were playing that evening and seeing us on stage looking so smart in suits and ties, composed and looking very professional, he told us that for the first time ever he felt proud to be connected with steel band,

Russel did not give much respite to his habit of drinking, initially taken up in Trinidad, he was extremely jolly when he had attained a certain intake of alcohol, and would soon sleep it off to wake up looking around him startled at his surroundings and at how he could have landed there.

We saw the end of all rationings in 1954.

Through our agent Paul, gigs were materialising, he booked us to play for a tea party given by Her Majesty the Queen Mother at Lambeth Palace.

When I spoke of our next engagement to an astonished Tony Kinsey who had been so judiciously teaching me on how to play the drums and that I wanted to 'roll' perfectly for the National Anthem, he was ready on the spot.

I must add that then, the Royal Family was considered untouchable, and highly respected, on an unapproachable pedestal, representing the all mighty. The title of Queen or King or of other members of the Royal Family still communicated the unreachable with a connotation of passed times, they were never the object of written scandals or mundane gossips, they seemed disconnected from the rest of the human race.

Of course for us playing for the Royal Family then, was an extraordinary opportunity.

On a sunny summer afternoon, we arrived on the south banks of the river Thames, at the striking Lambeth Palace, one of the few remaining medieval buildings in London. A butler led us to the garden, where a huge marquee was erected with a number of staff, in immaculate black and white outfits, busied themselves around beautifully laid white clothed tables and large silver dishes filled with sandwiches and cakes.

We set up our instruments under a tree where a piano had already been placed, a good distance from the marquee.

We played for the arrival of the guests until Her Majesty made her entrance. We then switched to the national anthem and I rolled and rolled after which, Russ, Max and I took up our steel drums which switched her Majesty's attention to the music, listening, she waved to a waiter who suddenly came rushing in our direction, flushed by the running and slightly shaken by the fact that he had been spoken to by the Queen:

"Her Majesty requests that you come a little closer."

Playing a waltz (the loveliest night of the year), with our pans around our necks, we walked towards the marquee to the royal table, she smiled and bowed her head to us when a sudden burst of applauses filled the tent.

This was 1955 and the beginning of many engagements for the Royal Family.

Over the years we performed at Windsor Castle when to our calypso music, the Queen Mother danced with Douglas Fairbanks Junior, swinging past us with a poised and delighted air.

At Goodwood House where, after the races, Lord Marsh, gave a barbeque for the entire Royal Family. During our break, the three of us walking around the garden and along a high hedgerow were startled when two men loomed out from the other side of the tall bushes taking us by surprise. Prince Philip seeing us in the distance walked towards us and addressing us:

"I saw that you all got surprised by these two men but you see when you give security men a job they make a meal out of it!"

He engaged the conversation on Trinidad he had visited and its innovative musical instrument.

I told him that back home the bands were much bigger to this he replied:

"The amount does not count I enjoy your trio very much!"

We performed at Princess Margaret's wedding, for Winston Churchill at Marlborough House who then was in a wheel chair; every year for the Cambridge and Oxford May balls when towards the end of the night, we came out onto the streets, still playing and leading all the students in their ball gowns and morning suits, dancing to the early morning hours."

The 50s was a prosperous decade for England, the reconstruction after the war was in full swing with the increase of manufacturing firms. The Festival of Britain also had enormous repercussion on modernisation and the emergence of consumer goods such as televisions, radios, washing machines, the expansion of offices and the introduction of new jobs.

Sterling Betancourt 1951 London

Fort George

Queen's house in 2012

Maywo 1948 playing mass with Crossfire

Sterling with his sister Sheila, Achilles Road 1964

Sterling's brother, Herman in train driver's uniform,
Mortimer Road 1959

Griffith conducting

The Russ Henderson Trio Sterling & Mervin Constantine
1954

Princess Margaret's wedding Marlborough house 1960
with Lady Ansen

Lord Mayor show 1961

Oxford debutant ball 1959

Bea and Benjamin 1975 (Inset Kat)

West Hampstead street parade

Sterling, Boogsie & Russ

Sterling, Benjamin, Clem, Sammy & Stefan

With Calypso singer Crazy & Tenor pan player Robert
Grenidge 1993

With A Williams and the Mayor M. Brown Trinidad 2006.

With Ellie Manette in France

With Frank Superville.at Notting Hill 2002

Benjamin & Brian 2011

With Brian Lara July 1999. World Cricket Cup

With (left) Sir Vivian Richards & Richie Richardson,
Cricketers 2009

Sterling giving Prince Charles his TASPO STORY
CD.May 2013

Buckingham Palace with Maminette 2001.four
generations!

Oetlishousen2_3_klein

The Angels with Sterling and Eliza

Playing with the Mariachis at Benjamin's 40th birthday party
September 2012.

Chapter XI
Mywo in London
1956

"I had saved up enough money to send back home for my mother to travel to London, she came in 1956 to stay in Ashmore Road with my brother who few months earlier had arrived from Trinidad and rented a room in the house in Maida Vale.

Herman had to leave his wife and children in Port of Spain waiting until he could save enough money for them to join him, he worked with the railway company and soon, after Mywo's arrival secured a job for her to work cleaning the carriages.

A year later my sister Sheila was to join us in London and obtained a job at the Stonebridge Park railway, her husband who would arrive the following year and likewise worked there as maintenance. The London rail network still provided work for many of the immigrants who were contributing in the maintenance and smooth running of public transport.

Russ and I in 1957, moved to Rawlings Street in Chelsea, I was then dating Sheila, a girl from Yorkshire, whom I had met at the Sunset Club one evening; she had arrived in London with all the hopes and dreams that the big city seemed to communicate to girls like her, in search of work, freedom and maybe love …

After few weeks, having found no jobs and no place to stay, she moved in with Russ and I, our relationship was brief but she got pregnant, abortion was out of question for her and I never completely knew if the purpose of her decision was justifiably the fear of a back street abortion, the hope of a marriage that would give her respite or that her upbringing in the 50s Yorkshire was so deeply imprinted in her that it overruled any other sense of practicality.

Did not you say the other day that, in fact, we are the product of our upbringing and education, a kind of doctrine?

If I did not approve of Sheila's decision, I could not force her into an act that she was so opposed to, even if we both knew very well that we were not in love with each other, that I was very engaged with music, with the work our band was obtaining, that our relationship had never been that serious. Despite all these negative points she fiercely hung on to her decision and baby Denise was born on the 28th March 1958 and we all welcomed her into our world with love, sincerely believing, in this inconsiderate state, that we were to give her all the care she needed.

Mywo had proposed to help us with the baby so Sheila, I and baby Denise moved in with her and Herman in Maida Vale in the unoccupied rooms left for rent.

We all seemed prepared to give Denise a home and a family.

I must have been deprived of all sense of perception, my involvement with the music and gigs I had been so desperate to achieve were in fact my world, there was so little room for Sheila's inconsequent behaviour as she became more uncontrollable when starting to date one of Herman's friend who had arrived from Trinidad and was living with us for a while.

Most evening I would be on gigs, touring different parts of the country, no-one in the house mentioned their doubts about Sheila's behaviour but I eventually became aware of it and mentioned it to her. Sheila blew her top and a very unpleasant argument followed, she was going to leave and take little Denise to an orphanage. Opposing her decision, Mywo and I told her that if she wanted to abandon Denise, we, without doubt would keep her with us, at least not depriving her of a real family, the fight went on for few days, Sheila had become vehemently against us and anyone who would disapprove of her resolution and used the fact that after all we were not married and Denise was a Massey and not a Betancourt.

She won in front of the authorities, and to our great dismay, Denise was taken to Barnardo's home in Tunbridge Wells.

Mywo, with the good intention to influence Sheila, made a few attempts to visit her in Yorkshire where she had returned, Sheila was adamant that she would never give us the rights to Denise.

Sheila never looked back on her daughter.

Mywo and I visited Denise in the orphanage and at six years of age she was sent to foster parents in Canterbury, to an English family who appeared to be caring, only when as a teenage girl Denise ran away did we think that something terribly wrong must have happened, she was subsequently taken to a remand home where we visited her."

How painful sometimes it is to glimpse back on some sensitive area of our lives, having stepped out of the situation and grasped clearly without all the emotion that blurs the vision, the extend of the malaise, the extent of our own defects.

"I had wondered if being West Indian then had weaken our situation in bringing up Denise.

In retrospect we could only blame ourselves for our lack of discernment.

The way Denise succeeded in giving her two sons so much love and care is for me a sign of how much she had, herself, suffered of having been denied and deprived at an early age of any form of affection, not to say love.

Her warmth and generosity must have been inherent to her genes and experience, granting her solace.

The same year Denise was born, our agent had organised for our Trio a series of variety shows all over England, sharing the bill with Frankie Howerd, Spike Mulligan, Connie Francis.

We had met Max's brother, Ralph who had just arrived from Trinidad, he played the bass and the steel drum, we became a quartet.

The shows were to start in Brixton, supposedly an area in London where mostly black people lived but for the week we performed there we did not see one black face in the audience!

Until then we had played in tropical patterned shirts and black trousers, the stage manager advised us that for the tour we should change our appearance and swap our traditional Caribbean style for a sharper and smarter image. We purchased red jackets, black trousers, white shirts, black ties and black patent shoes.

The England tour lasted many months, travelling by train sometimes staying overnight in the town of our performance, sometimes in London for few days, our quartet was a novelty, everywhere our music was always received with enthusiasm.

Also the same year, after Sheila's departure, I moved out of Ashmore Road to Bassett Road, W10, with Russel who then was renting one of the two basement flats at number 24. Like all the houses in Basset Road, number 24 was a large house with pillars holding the porch to the few steps up the main entrance, the large rooms had been converted into smaller ones and the owner, Dalton Brown, wanting to sell the property, asked Russ which would have proved to be an amazing investment!

To our detriment our heads were certainly not focused on any form of realism or future "

The poor end of Notting Hill stretched to the north of Ladbroke Grove to Harrow Road and Kensal Town, known as North Kensington. The area was inhabited by a pretty animated, stimulating and mixed crowd of, musicians, drug dealers, pimps, bohemians, rogues and misfits. An area inspiring writers and film makers alike, it is said to have been the epicentre of the British underground.

There was cheap housing, squats, crash pads and dubious slum landlords and their henchmen, Peter Rachman owned many squalid houses in the area, usually renting them to immigrant families who had nowhere else to go because of the racial context at the time. Rachman was himself a Jewish immigrant, who had escaped from Poland.

There were the 1958 riots with the Teddy Boys and in the 59 election, the end of the British fascist, Oswald Mosley.

Mixed couples were often the targets for those boys who moved around in groups for support, they often came from outside London, getting their kicks out of targeting black people who would often be singled out, the press might also have slightly exaggerated the small incidents, sparking off more racial tension.

In riots there is often a certain amount of people joining in without any actual conviction or passionate ideology....

"In Praed Street ,W2, 'The Trinidad Restaurant' was the meeting point for all West Indians, it was owned by a Chinese man from Guyana, Mooksan, who then moved the location to 127 Westbourne Park Road and named it the El Rio café. When Mooksan returned to Guyana, Frank Critchlow, who had been working with him since the 'Trinidad Restaurant', took over number 127.

(Back in Trinidad, Frank and his brother, Victor, had been at St Crispin School with me and for the first time since school days I will see them again working at the Trinidad Restaurant). Trinidadians and Jamaican met there eating chicken and rice while in the basement card games and gambling went on, a bell upstairs was used to warn the basement of an imminent raid in order to hide all the takings, on arrival the police would find innocent gamblers playing for fun.

The restaurant chef once cooked a pig snout soup, Zigglee, a steel band musician, who had ordered it, looked at his bowl shouting to the chef, "Bassa you could have at least blocked the pig's moustache!"

Christine Keeler and her entourage were visitors; it was well known to be a joint where prostitutes and their pimps hang out.

There was Michael de Freitas, a hustler from Trinidad and a front man for Peter Rachman, later on becoming a leader of the black power movement known as Michael X, (after Michael big X). Michael de Freitas was eventually hung for murder in Trinidad.

Marijuana and hashish was easily obtained in the area but drugs had always been around the music scene.

In the early sixties, Chris Blackwell established his Jamaican label, 'Island Records', in Basing Street, the most famous independent record company in history to divulgate the sounds of Jamaica.

Only in the late sixties Frank Critchlow opened the Mangrove in All Saints Road, the street was nicknamed 'the front line' by the West Indians, ,grass' was sold openly to any passer-by who would be asked if he wanted 'anything', certainly the police must have been notified not to get involved. Only years later the street was raided and cleaned up and cameras installed...

Later on Portobello Road saw, with the arrival of the hippie movement, an abundance of beads, kaftans, velvet jackets and trousers, fashionable items for sale and whiffs of patchouli essence mixed with ganga aroma amongst its fruit and vegetable stalls.

The All Saints Hall, known now as the Tabernacle, where at one point Pink Floyd performed, became the favour of the underground.

I think rock groups were the first to experiment with LSD.

North Kensington has somehow retained some of its cultural and class assortment that had made this area an exciting place to live in.

Fervently, Mywo, played the Littlewoods football pools with the conviction that one day her chance will come. Eventually, at the end of 1958, she won and with her practicality bought a house in Kensal Rise, I do not think that she ever was a football expert but she just struck lucky.

Since her arrival in London in 1956, she had made friends and with them would go to bingo and to church, and when possible she would come where we played, her love for music, dance and costumes always prevailed over any of the difficulties she experienced or had over the years, her answer to any problems was " never mind them ."

There was a lot to learn from her!

Every Sunday morning, between 12.30 and 2.30 pm, we played at the Colherne, at 261 Old Brompton Road, Earl's court, a pub, where all well-known jazz musicians met and 'had a blow', Dizzy Gillespie. Ronnie Scott, Tubby Hayes, Joe Harriet, John Surnam and many others. It was a sort of recreation, a meeting point for various ethnic groups from all social background. We played there until 1975, Russ on piano, Ralph on bass and I on drums, people called it 'the Sunday school'. There, years later, Russel was to meet his future wife, Marie.

It was our way of socialising with music, enjoying the sessions with other musicians who would join in with their own instrument, there was a fantastic atmosphere, smoky like hell, reeking of beer and other beverages, roties and black pudding were sold outside on the pavement where, for not having found space inside, a vast number of people hung out.

The habitués of the pub would arrive very early in the morning, buy all their drinks at once before the bar got so crowded that it became unapproachable and the chance to be served very slim.

Passers-by often stopped, asking what the attraction was.

A film was made of us playing there.

During the week, the Colherne was a famous meeting point for gays, few would come on Sundays but it was mostly a heterosexual crowd, another well-known spot for gays, was the Rockingham, a private club, where we also played every Sunday evenings from 1959 and for many years after.

It was on one of these Sunday mornings at the Colherne that I met Yolande.

Yolande Achong was born in Lancashire, raised in Trinidad, the daughter of a Trinidadian sportsman, Ellis Achong, nicknamed 'Puss', an excellent cricketer in the early 30s and the first Chinese man to play in a test match. Because of his peculiar way of bowling with his left arm unorthodox spin he was given the name of 'slow left arm Chinaman'.

He played for the West Indies against the English cricket team, after his last test match in 1935 he played for the Lancashire leagues until 1951, then returned to Trinidad.

Yolande who was accustomed at receiving a certain amount of recognition in Trinidad for being Atchong's daughter, felt slightly out of her depth in London not encountering the attention she was used to. She worked at the Citizen's Advice Bureau and often frequented the Colherne, meeting Russel and I, and soon enough became a regular at Bassett Road, we started dating.

Mywo then, was living in the house she had bought in Kensal Rise, my brother and sister Sheila had left Ashmore Road and moved in with my mother. Herman's wife had not yet arrived in London. I decided to move in with them and subsequently Yolande came to live with us.

Yolande became pregnant and wanted a child, she spoke of marriage and as the months went by the urgency became vital for her, marriage gradually became a matter of life and death, not to repeat the same predicament as with Sheila, so recent within me was the abandonment of Denise present in my mind, we got married in July at the Kensington Register Office and moved to a flat I rented in West Hampstead, Achilles Road.

Simon was born in October that year, three months later Yolande manifested her desire to take the baby to Trinidad for her family to see, she was homesick and longed to spend some time with her siblings in the warm climate. Candidly I thought that it would benefit her, far from imagining that I would never see her again.

Few weeks later, I received a letter from her just stating that she would not come back to Britain.

It is not in my intention to sound like a victim, on the contrary if I describe how I felt at reading the letter and say that the relief was immense, it will not depict a very compassionate or attractive image of myself, but it will be the truth.

Somehow I never worried about Simon, knowing that he will be well looked after by Yolande and her family, not like Sheila, Yolande would be responsible and caring.

The first time I met Simon was in 1976 when I visited Trinidad again.

I contemplated to strictly lead for the rest of my existence an absolute bachelor conduct.

Besides, our Russ Henderson Trio was totally absorbing our time with the numerous gigs.

Then the BBC radio organised a series of live shows to unite West Indian musicians from all different fields and without any past connection, we took part in the project that was to last for weeks, including the many rehearsals.

The challenge to perform with other musicians, playing music that was not in our repertoire that combined an extensive diversity of instruments, was an exciting experience we very much enjoyed.

We were also playing for television series, *The Saint*, *The Avengers, Danger Man* and for films like ,*'The Boy Who Talks To Animals'*, for the horror film *'Dr Terror's House of Horrors'*, starring Peter Cushing and Christopher Lee. We participated in TV programs like *Blue Peter, The Rolf Harris Show*...

Chapter XII
Achilles Road
The 60s

"Soon, my top floor flat at 43 Achilles Road, West Hampstead, became a refuge for the many Trinidadians who recently had arrived in the UK.

Never locked, 43, was also a meeting place and a recreation spot to 'lime & jam' for many Trinidadians, musicians and friends, also over the years I was to encounter, a constant stream of new faces, brought by friends and sometimes by friends of friends...

After having lived with my mother at Mortimer Road, my cooking had greatly improved.

I was now able to afford all the necessary ingredients to diversify the dishes I prepared and experimented on and enjoyed providing for my friends, knowing all too well how difficult it was yet for some to establish themselves, and estimated myself very fortunate to earn a living doing what I loved most. I knew that some even shop-lifted for their groceries, some even stole my milk from the front door step!

We would all get into jam sessions playing music, someone would pick up my guitar or the Congo drums or the instruments they came with and play well into the night, when on gigs I would frequently, on my return home, find the same friends I had left hours before, with a few additions and my fridge raided. My doorbell constantly rang, if no answer was obtained, number 41 where a friend of mine, Freddie, lived, would become the next target. Freddie was from Antigua and lived with his French girlfriend, Viviane, both became my close friends. Freddie played trap drums in his spare time, loved books and worked at the Maida Vale library, when he got too excited his stuttering became worse and added to even more frustration, always giving us the temptation to finish his sentences.

Ram John Holder, was a guitarist from Guyana and often 'jammed' with us, he played at the Moulin Rouge in Finchley Road where, after our gigs at the Habana off the main road, we would turn up to meet him. He recorded many albums, also worked as an actor in many films and television series.

Soon all the rooms at 43 Achilles Road were occupied by friends, and vacancies were never heard of, if someone left he was immediately replaced by someone I knew.

In the late sixties a sculptor and his wife, Andy and Stacy, took the ground floor flat left by Benito and his girlfriend, they worked in the garden giving it an artistic touch decorating it with some of his massive sculptures. Stacy was a little actress who succeeded in landing one of the leading part in the film *Two Anglaises et le Continent* (two English girls) by the famous French director, Francois Truffaud.

Stephen Kalipha, who I had met a few times since his arrival in 1959 while staying at a musician friend of mine in Stockwell, had expressed the desire to move closer to our area, he then for a couple of weeks moved in with Russel in Bassett Road until a room was vacant at 43.

The young Kalipha eventually enrolled at the Royal Academy of Dramatic Art, RADA, then, one of the most renowned drama schools in the world and pursued an accomplished career as a theatrical actor, in films and TV. He always had been interested in Buddhism and convinced it was the way of life he was most inclined to believe in, pursued in that direction and now gives lectures.

Shortly after, his cousin Horace Ove arrived, whose brother Valmont Jones, under the pretence of organising a show in Port of Spain with Sam Cook and after having collected the takings, had rapidly left Trinidad for England with all the money.

One of the songs of our calypsonian 'Sparrow' mentions 'bring back the fat man' speaking about Valmont, he was indeed very fat and very charming, his being in London did not eradicate the inclination he possessed for deceiving people, he eventually moved to the West End for more excitement and before he vacated his rented flat there, sold it as his own property and after such a coup, I think he left England to settle in Tobago where he ultimately died.

At a bus stop in West End Lane, Kalipha met a Guyanese, Sammy Devonish, looking at this smartly dressed boy made a comment on his suit, too happy to give some information on his fashionable outfit, Sammy engaged in a chat having already found out from Kalipha everything about us at Achilles Road where he became a regular and a friend. Sammy shared a house with his sister just around the corner, at Ulysses Road and worked as a pattern cutter for the West End fashion houses, Sammy loved clothes and was always smartly dressed, loved smart restaurants, champagne and most of all, like the rest of us, women.

For a short period, Irwin moved into 43 and now and then gigged with us, also played with the Original Limbo Dancers who had finally made the London trip and finished filming *Fire Down Below* with them. He performed at the famous Churchill Club in Bond Street and the Eve Club at 189 Regent Street, the same night running from one club to the other. While in Germany on tour with 'The Original Limbo Dancers' and before making their three weeks appearance at the Olympia in Paris, the Congo player decided to remain in Berlin having fallen in love. Irwin desperately phoned around for a replacement that at such a short notice was not easy to find. It was Russel who finally recommended Erol Philip, known as 'Blocker', who joined them in Paris (the source of his nickname as so far eluded me)....

After quitting the band, Irwin played with us for a while until he formed his own band 'Exotics' and toured Europe, then after many problematic years with his band he quit and toured Japan with Edmondo Ross.

Irwin is the only one of us who has mastered and spoke fluently four languages.

A cousin of mine, who I never had met in Trinidad, Tony Wilson, lived in a street behind Achilles Road, Ilfield Road, we became acquainted when mutual friends mentioned the family connection.

Tony also a musician, was the guitarist in the very popular band *Hot Chocolate*, Erol Brown the lead singer also lived in the same street and as we both had our heads shaven, his crowd of groupies evidently not knowing clearly his exact address and searching for him along our streets in West Hampstead caught a glimpse of my bald head one day, mistaking one for the other, ended on my doorsteps. Not until the giggling groupies were absolutely persuaded I was not Erol Brown, for a few days I was greeted by stare-eyed youths producing in me a scary feeling of anticipation when I was about to leave my house. I realised what it must be like on a larger scale to be famous, I thought it a kind of alienation. To control one's stardom must be quite a harrowing experience in order not to suffer from press harassment!

At the beginning you probably enjoy all the attention and when it is already too late to decide otherwise, you are caught up in the system

In the 80s when, in Abu Dhabi for a gig, I met Erol in the hotel lobby who was also giving a performance there, we caught up on past times, with some nostalgia he mentioned that my voice reminded him of his childhood days....

The early 60s were a busy time for our Trio, we performed most evening, touring many parts of the UK and Ireland, often privately flown over to play at some prestigious party, I still remember how the McCormick family were the most welcoming and appreciative clients and the best hosts we had encountered so far. I also remember, when on Lambey Island, I think it was privately owned, off the east coast of Ireland in the Irish Sea, we were taken to this greatly lit and grand stoned house where the guests seemed to fit so elegantly within that periodic background. There were so many grand evenings then, people really dressed up, it was dazzling.

The previous day when performing in Dublin at the Hibernian Hotel, one of the guest chatting with us told us how the IRA, already bombing in Belfast, would soon reach the streets of London.

On a boat trip to Dublin, the purpose of our journey has been erased from my memory but not the vivid picture of the few priests on that boat, very chatty and high on many Guinness, quite flushed, when their friendliness transpired to be too familiar to our liking we thought of keeping our distance and move on to a different spot, it ended by the three of us having to hide to escape their chasing us, of course it was just another excuse for laughter and making jokes!

Around the same time, after having passed my driving test, I bought my first car, a white Metropolitan, soon after, I drove to Italy to see my Italian girlfriend, Claudia, who I had met a year before when she was au pair in a family in Golders Green and when eventually she had to return home to Verona I visited her there. I drove through Switzerland making one stop in Zurich to see another girlfriend from earlier days then through the Alps to Italy, I never thought, when I studied the map, that it could be so far away!

After meeting Claudia in Verona, we drove to Venice, Milan and Paris and on the way back to England all the car tyres burst, I must have driven like a lunatic, the thought of having to check them did not even enter my mind, it was my first car after all...

Claudia and I saw each other for another couple of years, it was the longest relationship I ever had so far, she had found a permanent job and had her own flat, it suited us both for a while.

I can see how interested you are and how much you would like to ask me if it was a big love affair...what were my feelings for her and so on...I liked her, you are prompting me to say more but isn't liking her not strong it enough?"

I am always wondering if your feelings had been so restrained and concealed from an very early age as a protection or, if your emotions have always been so balanced, never tilting the scale one way or the other, like sailing above the sea regardless it is calm or rough or sunny or grey, your moods neither high or low, so it seems! Could it be a wisdom you have acquired?

It is quite baffling to discern what touches you deeply and the intensity of your feelings.

"Maybe it is a kind of natural disposition but over the many years I certainly have acquired a certain wisdom.

For Claudia, the idea of marriage was slowly gaining ground and it was clear that she needed some commitments for us to really be together, our views separated us, I was contented to carry on as it was and as long as it lasted, I did not think, from previous experience, that we needed to rush to such an important decision and could not fathom the idea of living together yet. I thought that time was in our favour anyway.

We broke up and we never saw each other again. I think she returned to Italy.

And life went on.

We were working every evening at the Beachcomber in Mayfair, I think I have already spoke about that club, at the piano Boscoe Holder, his wife Sheila as the vocalist, Irwin on double bass and I on the drums, I have kept a coloured picture of us playing there.

Russel and I sometimes had to share some of the gigs and now and then worked solo on piano.

148

For the first time since I had left Trinidad, I returned in 1964, for a very short stay."

The Trinidad prime minister then, was Dr Eric Eustace Williams, descendant of a French Creole family on his mother's side, he had successfully won a scholarship and studied at Oxford where he graduated in History.

In the course of his life he had written many books and given many lectures. After having lived and worked in America, he returned to Trinidad in 1948 to follow a political career and in the meantime developed an important position in politics, giving a series of lectures to eventually create his own party, the 'Political Education Movement' (PEM) finally launching in 1955 the PNM (Political National Movement). He won the 1956 general elections that led to the independence of Trinidad in April 1962 and in 1966 the PNM won the majority of votes.

In 1963, Martin Luther King gave a speech in Washington and said "I had a dream." one of the most important moment for the civil rights movement and quest for racial equality.

"Williams, after attending a conference in Africa, flew back to England and before heading back to Trinidad notified that seats were available on his plane to give Trinidadians living in London the opportunity to visit their country during the carnival week end for the very modest fare of £60 return.

I of course booked two tickets for me and my mother, my brother and sister with their respective spouses came too and naturally on the flight were many familiar faces and courtesy of the Prime Minister there was Champagne for everyone.

Thirteen years had elapsed since my departure from port of Spain, it felt good to be back even for such a short stay, I visited my old band 'Crossfire' and other steel bands, some members of the original TASPO had joined different bands.

TASPO had not survived, only a vivid memory to these days!

In the pan yards, the old rusty drums had been replaced by chromed pans, they were played with metal sticks with a rubber on its tip.

While, at the 'Crossfire' pan yard I heard the menacing voice of Rudolph Bodoo, nicknamed Ghandi for his slight frame, asking around who had stolen his sailor hat, looking very threatening indeed with, in his hand a cutlass wrapped up in a newspaper, I was slightly concerned at first, and tried to pacify him as my time in England had led me to forget that these performances were not to be taken too seriously.

Only thirteen years away and it felt as if half a century had passed.

On the Tuesday the last day of carnival, I saw bottles flying over people's heads, a good indication that a fight was just about to start, just as it used to be, after all nothing really had changed.

When on the plane that same evening it felt good to go back to London.

Kay was a friend with a music agency, handling rock bands like Danny Williams, Hot Chocolate, and few others, to help her out around the house and at work she had French au pairs. Succeeding each other there was, Evy, followed by

150

Katia and last Janine, all to become friends of ours. When their year contract ended and they returned to Paris to eventually work for a record company they maintained a close contact with us all and made many trips to London for weekends or short breaks, most of the time at Achilles Road, despite my small flat. They hung out with us, came to the parties, to the Colhern and at Danny Williams who lived opposite the pub in Earls Court.

The parties were wild, with marijuana joints repeatedly passing, hashish cakes, sometimes coke and LSD, sometimes mixed in food you would not be aware of, but as a rule I always tried to be cautious with party food after having been caught once. My experience had left me dubious after having sat all night watching a light bulb changing size and colour, it was not such a fulfilling vision that I ever wanted to repeat.

I preferred smoking marijuana and hash.

I was already in my early 30s when I had my first smoke, these were the 60s, the flower power, the youth phenomenon, the cultural revolution, swinging London, the Beatles, the Rolling stones….Carnaby Street and Kings Road, it was said that London was the most exciting city! The wild fashion, Mary Quant and Biba, Shrimpton, Twiggy and her mentor Justin de Villeneuve, Mr Freedom, the film *Blow Up* by Antonioni."

By then the Mod sub-culture movement with the R&B and pop music, Italian scooters, tailor made suits and dandies slowly went into decline with the Hippie culture taking over.

Also the Labour Government came into power with Wilson in 1964:

The Labour years of Britain!

Before the hippie movement coming from the United States in the mid-60s to oppose the US military intervention in Vietnam, there was in 1960, the 'Ban the Bomb' demonstrations in London, starting at Trafalgar Square.

"The largest demonstration that London had seen so far, it was an anti-nuclear protest against the building of nuclear power station in Britain, we joined and played, marching with our steel band around our neck."

The famous peace symbol that was adopted by the hippies in America, was originally designed in Britain for that Nuclear disarmament campaign!

The peace symbol, the most recognised symbol of all with the swastika!

The hippie movement was so powerful that its influence and significance still reverberate in the 21st century!

"We are now in the flower power era, the late sixties, when Katia, Evy and Janine brought with them another French girl, the beautiful 21 year old Katherine.

Working in the same building, in Paris, they frequently saw each other by using the same lift, and gradually by exchanging greetings they engaged in conversation. Katherine then heard them comment on the fun week ends they were all having in London, she eventually was convinced to accompany them on their next trip.

This is how I met Katherine.

All the boys became very agitated and chased her with much ardour, but without success, Katherine had a boyfriend in Paris she very much loved.

Sammy, so infatuated he was with her that he even wanted to marry her!

The attention that all girls received, made them feel very special not realising at the time that it was a very short lived experience until another interest would come along.

I liked Janine she was my girlfriend at the time.

Katherine spent many week-ends in London, enjoying the fashion and the Kensington shops, Biba, Bus Stop, immersing herself in the fascinating atmosphere that seemed to constantly prevail, the music at the Colherne or the Rockingham, the parties, there were always parties then and the carnival.".…

Was the first Notting Hill carnival in 1965?

Chapter XIII
The Notting Hill Carnival

"Trinidad born Claudia Jones was raised in New York and there became a member of the communist party and a strong defendant for the black community. After having worked at the Daily Worker newspaper as the editor and giving speeches on human and civil rights, she was considered controversial and during the McCarthy period was imprisoned and in the mid-fifties deported.

After having been granted asylum in the UK she settled in London and founded *The West Indian Gazette*, an Afro Asian Caribbean and anti-racist newspaper.

At the St Pancras Town Hall in January 1959, she organised an indoor Caribbean cabaret for the mardi gras celebration directed by Edric Connor which our steel band played for and actually was filmed by the BBC television.

Also in the Kensington Town Hall was held a sort of Caribbean festival.

But the really first Caribbean outdoor festival took place in 1964, in, Notting Dale, when Rhaune Laslett, who lived in Acklam Road, W10, and Andre Shervington, a Guyanese, (we had known since the 50s at the Sunset Club) both community activist and social workers, decided to organise a children's carnival in the poorer and deprived end of Notting Hill, (north Kensington area of today) with the intention of drawing together the ethnic groups when racial tension still subsisted.

Rhaune and Andre, who knew of our steel band, asked us, "The Russ Henderson Steel Band", to play for a children's event they were organising on a Sunday in June. Following our usual session at the Colherne, we arrived in Acklam Road bringing with us a little crowd from the pub always in search of some new and exciting entertainment.

Rhaune had borrowed donkey carts and floats from the fire brigade, the children were all dressed up in fancy dress and painted faces, we started playing at the corner of Acklam Road and Portobello Road, friends, children and parents dancing to our music, when Russel suggested to take a road march while playing, with our drums around our necks. The crowd followed.

This road march took us from Portobello Road to Westbourne Grove and via Chepstow Road onto Notting Hill and Holland Park Avenue. When passing the police station in Ladbroke Grove, we saw many policemen gathering behind the windows, bewildered and looking at the crowd not knowing what was going on or what to do!

A crowd of hundreds, people who had joined us on the way, followed the band dancing, clapping and sometimes from the pavement where many onlookers stood staring, a shout could be heard: "Why don't you go back to your bloody country what are you demonstrating about!"

Some associated our playing with the CND demonstration marches, which we had joined and played for walking from Kensington to the West End.

Ginger Johnson, had also come to the children festival and play his African drums made from an elephant foot; big

George, from Grenada, who worked as a doorman in Mayfair, who never would have missed a Sunday morning at the Colherne beating his iron piece, was there with his metal can.

We all walked dancing for few hours, people coming from church in their best dress, with hats and bags in hand swinging to the rhythm, West Indians wining as if they felt such a release at this unexpected glimpse of their well missed carnival culture.

The Notting Hill Carnival was born.

At the 1965 children's festival we decided to change the route and deviate to Porchester Road to entertain the bedridden wife of our bass player, Fitzroy Coleman, who could see the band through the windows, and enjoy the music. More people were seen on the road but we remained the only steel band.

Every year we witnessed how the crowd increased and how not only children wore costumes but gradually adults too.

I always thought that, in Acklam Road, should stand a bust of Rhaune Laslett and Andre Shervington for they pioneered one of the first multi-cultural event in Europe, bringing over two million people from all over the world, never could they have guessed then, the escalating scale of their decision, neither did we think that this small neighbourhood children's festival will become Europe's biggest!

The carnival was eventually moved from June to the August bank holiday, at first it was very much a steel band and African drum affair before the DJs trucks appeared.

Many people claimed having had an important role in initiating the Notting Hill Carnival but certainly, many contributions were made for its development and what it has become today; Claudia Jones, the late Selwyn Baptist, Leslie Palmer, Victor Critchlow, Claire Holder to name a few but the creative idea can only be attributed to Lasslett and Shervington.

When Rhaune Lasslett died in 2002. Russ, Herman and I played at her funeral.

When in the summer of 1967 we played at the Glyndebourne Festival Opera in East Sussex, on arrival we were sent to the wardrobe department to be fitted with period costumes and white wigs, it gave us ideas for our next carnival...

In1968 we recorded a calypso-jazz album with, John Surman on baritone sax, Mike Osborn on alto sax, Russ on piano, Dave Holland on bass and me on drums. John lived in Basset Road, we had sessions together and from this it was decided that we would all make a calypso-jazz record and at the following Notting Hill Carnival we joined forces and they all came on the road with us.

The following year in 1969, at the Notting Hill Carnival, we were the biggest band and for the first time had costumes made by my mother, and as the tradition goes, we played fancy sailors.

As I already mentioned, the 'Fancy American Sailor' masquerade goes back as far as the First World War when Trinidad was visited by many military men, French, German, English and American sailors, the natives mimicking the drunken sailors, mostly the Americans, then created the sailor dance.

Mywo had made great costumes and many of us were wearing the fancy sailor apparel, friend's children were also dressed, they gathered a jubilant crowd as they performed without inhibition their own interpretation of the fancy sailor dance, they were a great success and a joy to see.

From then on other bands came in costumes.

I think that we saw other bands joining in around 1968.

The costume designer and mass maker, Ashton Charles, brought out themes on the road soon followed by other mass makers. In 1970 he designed a medieval theme 'twelve century' for our steel band.

Mywo, Ashton Charles and I, had plans for Beatrice to be part of the medieval theme and before she knew it she was in a costume, we did not take her refusal too seriously, she most probably realised the opposition was too complex to endure and at the same time did not want to let us all down...

There is a picture of her and little Benjamin looking pretty miserable, I remember that she could not get out of her costume fast enough and go home...carnival is definitely not in her blood or any kind of exhibitionism. I think she prefers the behind the scene experience and creativity.

Years later she designed some of our band's costumes!

I should mention how we two have met."

Chapter XIV
Beatrice and Benjamin

When meeting Sterling in the mid-1970s, I did not immediately connect with Beatrice. Their son Benjamin, was then about four years old and Beatrice always seemed to keep Sterling's friends at a fair distance from her world.

I have over the years, gradually managed to be friends with both and a frequent visitor at their London home, witnessing the love that surrounded Benjamin and the growing up of this attractive individual, made a strong and everlasting impression on me.

When last year I decided to write Sterling's biography with Beatrice's support, she insisted that she should only be mentioned when really necessary and only when relevant to depict Sterling's personality, feelings that could only be perceived by the closeness and understanding of each other's character, or significant events in relation to him..

"After all it is to be Sterling's musical history not a novel and if we were to talk about the forty years we spent together you will need to write a few more books," said Beatrice.

Beatrice, Katherine's little sister, came to London in the autumn of 1969 to study. She was staying with a family in

Southgate, more precisely 'Hadley Wood', where she said having felt terribly lost, lonely and home-sick.

She had met Sterling through her sister who had described him as "The nicest man she had met so far and totally trustworthy, that he would chaperone her," repeatedly insisting that she should come out of her environment to meet different people.

Sterling recalls this time laughing:

"I had been waiting for her to call, Katherine had briefed me on how she felt and thought that, by meeting me, it would give her a chance to mix in a more cheerful atmosphere and when she finally called I realised that her English was really poor and when in the course of a couple of weeks, we planned to meet twice outside her school and failed, I thought better of it and next, chanced on Southgate tube station for an ultimate encounter.

We both arrived early for different reasons, I wanted to make sure that I would be more than on time and Beatrice had tucked herself away in a corner thinking of catching a glimpse of me before deciding to show up!

When I saw this young girl it was easy to guess she was Katherine's little sister, really shy, I took her to Achilles Road to some food I had cooked and meet friends who were there, Beatrice was looking at everything and everyone with wide opened eyes."

"When Sterling met me at Southgate tube station, leading me to his car holding my hand, it was, for me such an act of intimacy that I was taken aback and obviously straight away put up defences!" said Beatrice.

"I held your hand as not to look as if we were strangers meeting in a station! It was without any hidden intentions behind it, you were Katherine's little sister who I had promised to take care of!"

Beatrice:

"Since my arrival in London, a couple of months before, I was probably walking around with wide open eyes trying to grasp what was happening around me and to me, also the fact that my English was practically non-existent to hold any form of conversation, making enormous efforts to comprehend the words thrown at me, my eyes might have reflected the strain at guessing more than understanding what was said to me and, I had not until then, seen men in fake snakeskin trousers with frilly purple shirt, knitted bright coloured hat and patchwork jacket, the way Sterling favoured in dressing himself then!

The art school influence had not yet enough time to achieve injecting its multifaceted culture, neither I had ever lived in suburbia before confronted with very straight people as was the family I was staying with. I was extending my knowledge from one end of convention to the other of non-convention, a lot to deal with and apart from all this, I had rather be home in the country with my dog.

I remembered walking into Sterling's living room with its orange, square cushioned, L shape seat built along the corner of the wall with one side under the window and the two sections separated by a cube like table with a lamp, the 60s orange wallpaper with circles, the ever so huge aquarium with the beautiful tropical fishes and plants, the leather

African cushions on the orange carpet and the low table decorated with tiny squares of different shades of blue ceramics, that a friend had specially made for him. On the wall, a big poster representing the head of a black girl with Afro hair style with the mention 'Black is beautiful and its beautiful to be black', a portrait of Marsha Hunt perhaps and a colourful painting of a tropical scenery.

Through the kitchen window, in the adjacent room, Sterling, his hands resting on the worktop would call his friend Freddie who lived in the opposite house, they both had a way of calling each other by a distinctive whistling. The bedroom was a few steps down with on the mantelpiece bottles of cologne, with names like Brut and Old Spice aftershave!

I was to discover how Sterling was considerate and attentive to the well-being of his friends with an unequalled generosity and a nonchalant and carefree attitude he seemed to possess in approaching life and its challenges making everything appearing effortless, a deeply rooted trait in his personality. I was also to witness the facility with which he embraced, with an equal acceptance and with the same serene attitude whatever came his way or whoever crossed his path, with what seemed a total detachment.

His mother, Mywo, used to say that when you have to do something pleasant or unpleasant do not brood about it just get it over with otherwise it will be in your head all the time and it will end up absorbing all your energy.

On my visits to Achilles Road, I gradually met Sterling's friends and acquaintances who were passing through and sometimes staying, it was a foreign world to me and at the same time appealing to my need of escaping reality. After having spent Christmas at home in France, I came back with a friend from boarding school and camped in Sterling's flat until a room in the house next door became vacant.

My frustration at feeling mentally restricted and confined in an environment that certainly did not suit me had driven my endurance to its limits and after having spent the day in town, Sterling, considerately, drove me back to Hadley Wood stopping, as he always did at the nearest corner from the house, despite my insistence and laughs at his being too conscious, he would just point out that it was preferable that I was not seen with a black man.

Evidently, when that evening I insisted that he should drive closer to the house, he reluctantly did so and walking in the entrance hall, I was greeted with an indignant voice "But your friend Sterling is black!"

We were in 1970 and a couple of days later I was camping in Sterling's living room until my departure for France."

Beatrice eventually came back to stay .

Chapter XV
Mwyo's death
The 70s

Like many Trinidadian, Selwyn Mcsween immigrated to Canada after the immigration regulation of 1967 ending the White Canada policy.

Selwyn came to London to complete his law degrees, another steel band lover who also played the clarinet.

"I was really impressed when I first met him and heard his tenor pan, unlike the drums I had heard in London the sound of this one was much clearer, louder and much more harmonious than the usual pan, its notes had octaves, Selwyn also played with four sticks, two in each hand.

I learned that Patrick Arnold, a Tobagonian, was responsible for the tuning of that tenor pan, of course it became essential for me to acquire a similar drum, Selwyn ordered a couple for me, I gave one to Russel.

Only years later I was to meet Patrick Arnold, still living in Tobago and still tuning, he had then formed a band ,,

'Our Boys', and later on became the president for the Steel Pan organisation, 'Pantrinbago' dedicated to the worldwide promotion and development of the steel pan and pannists.

Subsequently, when in 1976 I received my first contracts to perform in Switzerland, Selwyn, stood in for me at the London Sheraton Hotel where I was under contract.

Then we lost contact after his return to Canada to practice law, presiding for the Ontario human rights at York University, I have heard that he also arranges music and conducts steel band classes!

I was making drums for the Elmwood junior school in Croydon and Russel taught the rudiments of music on the pan; James Cummings, a community relation officer in Croydon who knew the headmistress, approached an engineering firm to produce steel drums on a greater scale and at a quicker pace that I alone could not achieve. We thought it a great project involving us both, Russel and I but somehow when we approached Trinidad with this concept, it was unpleasantly received, importing drums from England to Trinidad the home of the steel band, was totally unacceptable. Funding also became a problem and unfortunately the project had to be aborted.

I accepted a contract with the recently opened, Skyline Hotel to play five evening a week, Russel was also offered to play piano few nights a week at Morton, Ralph had recently left us to form his own band and was replaced by the steel band players who were available at the time. Now and then someone had to stand in for me at the Skyline when other gigs necessitated my presence.

We did many fundraising and charity work, notably in 1973/74 we worked for the original 'Across' Jumbulance trust to make travel possible for disabled, notably to Lourdes in France, the events we played for were hosted by the late Jimmy Savile, also known for his 'Clunk Click' ad to persuade people of wearing seat belts! A slogan that became so well recognised and associated with J.Savile's TV show "Jim'll fix it" and his yellow hair...little did we know then, that after his death in 2011 a series of child abuse allegations would tarnish his OBE!

And for our recreation we played every summer at the Notting Hill Carnival and on Sunday, after having given up the Colherne, I played the steel drum at The Duke of Clarence in Holland Park with Ralph Cherrie and Benito Hernendez, there again every Sunday was a reunion of many steel band music fans and others.

After my six weeks trip to Trinidad and Tobago in 1977 with Beatrice and Benjamin, my introduction to Switzerland came through 'Blocker' whom I have known since the 50s. He had mentioned that the Nova Park Hotel in Zurich was searching for a steel band with a singer, I thought it might be interesting to bring steel band music to a country where it had not yet spread and the Nova Park ,built in 1972, was at that time, the biggest hotel in Zurich attracting a cosmopolitan and sophisticated clientele.

It will be my first trip to Zurich, eventually followed by many others.

Russel could not leave London then and would have to replace me for the gigs during that summer.

Soon after the audition, that had taken place in London, the three months contract was signed, we brought Melina Bascombe from Trinidad to be our vocalist.

I decided to drive to Switzerland where I would most probably need some transportation and to carry all the tools I usually have with me for tuning the pans.

We played every evening in the tropical garden where a Caribbean stage was erected, and, over the three months I played there, I made many contacts with Swiss enthusiasts, who, for the first time, were discovering steel band music, we became a huge attraction.

Soon the demands for drums were materializing and at such a pace that every afternoon, I would drive to the outskirts of Zurich, to a desolate field by a railway in Berminsdorf, with, in the back of my car ,an oil drum that I had picked up on a building site. The noise that derives from the making and tuning a drum is quite deafening and as I started to pound away on the drum with a hammer and steel punch, drivers on the distant road were slowing down looking in my direction, bewildered.

It must have been a strange sight, me in my vest, pounding on some sort of container making a hell of a noise that must have resounded in the distance! Once, two policemen showed up and slowly walking across the field to investigate what I could be up to, asked for my passport and work permit which wisely I always carried with me, having been advised to do so...I explained what I was doing and only when seeing my tenor pan in the back of my car did they understand and drove away. When, later on I narrated the incident, I was told that in Switzerland people often inform on each other, let alone on a black man in a vest pounding on an unidentified object!

From a building site nearby, workers had watched the scene obviously waiting for the policemen to depart to come over, offering me a space on their plot so I will not have to worry of being disturbed anymore and thanks to them I made many drums there.

It was during that first summer at Nova Park that I met Robert Hauser, a drummer from Zurich passionate with folk art, who, when finding out that a steel band was performing at Nova Park, came one evening to hear us and on one of our breaks introduced himself and his friend Franco Georgetti, a photographer, who expressed his desire to learn the steel drum and to acquire a pan.

Few years later, Franco formed his own band, 'Pink Floyd' who later on was named 'Sandflo', one of the best single pan steel band then in Zurich.

Robert organised a steel band workshops where I taught children and made small drums for them to learn on, I also made pans for a music store in Zurich, 'Music Hug" and gave private lessons.

In 1979, after my return with Beatrice and Benjamin from Switzerland, an unwell Mayo greeted us. She did not want to worry us while abroad, that over the last month she had been in pain and after the few visits she had made to her GP in Queen's Park, she had been diagnosed as having minor gastric problems and was sent home to rest.

When we saw her we knew by the colour of her skin that she was more than unwell, we took her to our doctor in King's Cross. (we were then living in Bloomsbury).

Dr Pitt certainly was not the usual general practitioner one is accustomed to as he put his mind and soul to every patient and was the most dedicated and considerate doctor we ever met or had. Sometimes we sat there waiting in his practice for hours, in order for him to give every patient the necessary time to be seen. From the waiting room you could just hear the muffled sound of his voice on and on...In 1975 he had been appointed to the House of Lords, by Harold

Wilson as Lord Pitt of Hampstead and granted a life peerage for spending his life speaking for the black community, he was the first West Indian to have a seat in parliament"

.

Pitt was born in Grenada and studied medicine in Edinburgh, after having graduated with honours he left England to practice in Trinidad, there he helped found the West Indian National Party, a radical party campaigning for the independence of the island.

In the late 1940s he came back to England to establish a London practice and continued to be very involved in fighting for the black community against discrimination and prejudice. He also became the president of the British Medical Association, a title that he was very proud of.

He remained in London until his death in the late 80s.

"After seeing Mywo, Dr Pitt was lost in thought, one hand rubbing his chin, there was a great silence in the room, then shaking his head he asked us, Beatrice, I and little Benjamin, to leave the room to speak alone to my mother.

Three weeks later Mywo died of cancer in hospital.

The cancer had spread all over her body and the morphine was soon taking its toll and after a week, she slowly stopped talking and would just lie there, the white of her eyes half showing under their lids now and then making some faint sounds, sometimes her eyes would open and stare at you with a flick of recognition, giving us the consoling thought that she might have seen us there with her. Her eyes closed, we would carry on speaking to her, telling her what we were doing, hoping she could hear our voices if not understanding us. The evening before her death, Mywo briefly opened her eyes and extended her hand towards me, who was sitting close to her; taken by surprise I reached out to hold her hand while the ring she always wore fell from her fingers into my hand.

The ring has never left me."

"I really feel that in leaving us, the dead steal a little bit of our soul, we all have experienced it and somehow each time, each death, takes away a portion of our youth.

As the one we cared for and loved die and we encounter death, some of our innocence fades away too."

Chapter XVI
Switzerland
More steel band than snow

After a visit to Trinidad, Robert spoke of a young steel band player he had met there, Andy Narell, showing me a picture of him holding a drum made by Ellie Mannette. Many years later Andy, a talented player, and I, were to meet in Switzerland.

The contract at the Nova Park was renewed every summer for six consecutive years, various players came to play with me there.

I made many acquaintances and many drums, taught many people who later formed their own bands, accepted private gigs, parties, venues, charity shows.

Switzerland had become the workforce.

Over the Christmas festivities, I would busk in many Swiss cities, my brother would join me for that period or other friends from London, not only for the extra francs that we always collected and appreciated but also for the pleasure of performing in the streets, a strangely rooted need in me.

On a Christmas Eve in Bern, after having collected about £3000 the three of us approaching a friend's flat, then realised that none of us was carrying the money bag that had been left at the bus stop, containing not only the takings of that day, but all my tapes.

We informed the police without having high expectation that someone's honesty would prevail over their needs or the temptation at seeing the cash.

But the following day to our astonishment, a Spanish lady who had heard us on the street had found the bag and its content at the bus stop, understood who the owners were and from the leaflets got our phone number.

A bag left at a bus stop then, did not provoke the fear that was to be experienced years later.

We were in awe and thanking her over the phone she just declared that if in the same situation she would have been grateful for a little integrity.

Busking again in Geneva wearing Santa Claus hats, we felt uneasy when a dozen policemen walking towards us asked if we had any hats to sell, since our permit did not allow selling goods, my CDs and the few hats concealed, we of course denied. Laughing and joking they insisted, finally I gave in to their persistence and sold them the rest of our hats.

Half an hour later they were to return dancing with their hats on and a camera, we had to pose with the twelve of them.

Busking in the streets often channelled new gigs and new contacts from all different level of society; once a car stopped along the pavement, a chauffeur in full livery came out towards us holding a note with written on it a request for us to play for a new year's private party in Gstaad."

Beatrice often mentions how Sterling was a man of the streets, that the streets were his roots and the place where he is most happy playing.

"Eventually Russel came to Nova Park and played piano in the lounge bar, despite my going away to Zurich, we would still performed together in London and enjoy in the summer playing with our band at the Notting Hill Carnival. There were always first time players, wanting to learn and join the band and I would organise workshops to teach them, a purely benevolent act satisfying the lingering keenness, need and desire to introduce steel band to new people, though I never succeeded with my son Benjamin!

All this time our carnival band had no name and I had been thinking, without having made much progress, of a distinctive epithet to describe our traditional pan around the neck band.

The twenty or more players were to rehearse during the months preceding the carnival in our practising hall, which over the years, moved to different addresses in North Kensington.

It was to be at Selwyn Baptiste in Powis Square, that the name for our band came up in 1985.

'Liming' there with few friends and mentioning how I had been searching for a suitable name for the band, it was 'Boots', Philmore Davidson a TASPO player, who while tapping his feet on the ground came up with the name 'Nostalgia'. The sound of it was sweet to my ears it perfectly described and represented our traditional pan around the neck, without a moment of hesitation my mind was made up, I remember leaving Powis Square in an elated state of mind.

For the 1985 carnival, Shell offered to sponsor Nostalgia, most of us appreciated the fact that we could receive some funds to build up the band and acquiring newer drums, when the late Frank Critchlow (the Mangrove owner) and his anti-apartheid activists threatened us not to even consider the Shell offer, being blood money. After some hesitation we turned down the proposal as some members of Nostalgia thought it wise not to get involved in any hazardous predicament with people who, in the past, had not always respected such an ethical attitude.

It sometimes is astonishing how righteousness emerges out of the men who often have a lot to answer for themselves!

The following year, in 1986, we got sponsored by Virgin who few months later hired Nostalgia (Russ, Junior Gill, Castro, Herman and myself) to play for the inaugural flight to Miami on which Richard Bronson held a champagne party, dancing to the sound of the steel band, forming a Congo line seven miles up in the air, the ambiance was fantastic!

Since the beginning of the 1980s I fulfilled a series of long contracts in various countries, Saudi Arabia, Oman, the United Arab Emirates, Qatar, Indonesia, Honk Kong, Macau, Morocco, etc… I would be then away for six to eight months at a time and in between there was London and of course, Zurich where, in the meantime, had occurred a rapid arrivals of pan players and tuners.

Steel band was spreading all over the Alps.

It inspired me to write a calypso song I eventually recorded in Trinidad:

'More Steel Band Than Snow'.

In 1987, coming back from my long contracts abroad in time to participate at the February Zurich carnival I was to meet again all the acquaintances and friends I had left few years before, now with their own pan around the neck steel band. The little 'Pink Floyd' had grown into the larger 'Sandflo', many pan tuners, pan makers, players from the UK and the West Indies had flocked to the city in search of new commitments and fortunately the contacts I had made over the years in Switzerland contributed to outspread the talent of my steel band friends.

I taught Sandflo to play the tune 'Kuchilala' which happened to be a great addition to the build-up of the Zurich carnival atmosphere that February,

I then thought of inviting them to join Nostalgia at the next London Notting Hill Carnival. At the mention of this, Sandflo showed their doubt at not being good enough players to fit in with Nostalgia, I proposed to teach them all the tunes we played and the new ones and for the next few months I became again, a much appreciated customer with Swiss Air.

In London the Nostalgia players were showing their discontent at sharing Nostalgia with a Swiss band, some even refused to play, I could not persuade them to understand that it could only be to a great advantage.

Every year during the Notting Hill Carnival weekend a tradition had been established for all the players to meet at my house and to start our carnival route from there on both mornings. The usually quite street became very lively with players unloading their drums setting up the small three wheels float, to accommodate the bass and amplifiers, with a constant traffic in and out of the house for a cup of coffee or a glass of rum.

When Sandflo joined us, adding to the amount of the Nostalgia players, the crowd in the house and the continuous comings and goings soon became overpowering and Beatrice first goodwill turned into anticipated anguish and exasperation, while Benjamin and Russel's younger son Pablo, taking the opportunity of the constantly opened door and the street activities would run amok.

Sandflo enjoyed the carnival enormously, the experience had left a very positive impact on both bands, it generated Sandflo's decision to improve and practise on a regular basis and widen their repertoire to come back the following year, in fact their dedication and discipline contributed in becoming the backbone of Nostalgia and a well-recognised pan around the neck steel band in Zurich.

They came back every year. When my contract in Morocco prevented me from rehearsing Sandflo to attend the 1988 Notting Hill Carnival, I asked a young talented Nostalgia player, Junior Gill, to replace me in Zurich and teach them the new tunes. Junior was later to establish his permanent residence in Zurich, creating a steel band school and touring the world with Billie Cobbham the great jazz musician, I never miss an opportunity to hear them perform at Ronnie Scott.

Staying at a friend Werner Schmidt, who lived close to a church in Zurich, early one morning in a half asleep state, I heard the church bell chime and was so suddenly transported to a particular era of my childhood in Trinidad, an episode that, until now, had never resurfaced to my consciousness, only to be awaken by the sound of these bells.

The experience seemed so real, not only for the visual memories but for a distinctive quality in the air and scents surrounding me then, I was really there, the pervading mood of the whole atmosphere in its minute details:

I was on my way back from church, at the foot of Laventille Road, when passing the corner I saw the Spiritual Baptist standing there all dressed in white having their prayer meeting, singing hymns evoking the spirit half in a trance, now and then ringing a bell. Around them, on the dusty pavement candles were burning and in a glass bowl flowers floating in water.

I could smell the candles and see the white delicate flower petals.

The Baptists were persecuted by the authorities and their practice (an afro Caribbean religion) was forbidden until 1951, as a young boy, this information must have contributed to the impact the whole scene had left in me, only resurging a decade later with the bell chimes.

In Zurich that morning I got up singing and wrote the lyrics for ,Sanky Soccer' which I recorded again in Port Of Spain, when in 1996, the Baptists faith was granted a public holiday by the Trinidad government and celebrated on the 30th March (my birthday), called the Spiritual Baptist Shouter Liberation Day.

Trinidad is the only country that gave it a public holiday.

The origin of the epithet 'Shouter Baptists' came from the clapping and shouting they create when catching the spirit.

Chapter XVII
La Creole/1991

Sterling was to return to Trinidad for the 1991 carnival, fourteen years after his last trip with Beatrice and Benjamin in 1977. Inviting his keen steel band friends, Werner Schmidt and his wife to the birthplace of the steel pan with the intention to also take a break and connect again with old acquaintances, family relatives and immerse himself in the musical atmosphere of the pan yards.

The few weeks prior to carnival and to the steel band competition is what Sterling enjoys most; when all the bands are rehearsing every evening in their own pan yards he would walk from one to the next listening to the new tunes, watching a new generation exploding with energy and talent.

Of course he would eventually get involved with music and during his 1991 trip it was to be with a pan around the neck band, La Creole Pan Grove, that he was asked to arrange a tune for the Panorama competition after having met accidently Derek, their PR.

The members of the band were of the new generation and never had heard of Sterling Betancourt, therefore thought very strange that they should be taught to play by someone from England and a few derogatory remarks were made, mentioning that THEY should teach him how to play. Only when Derek's father heard that Betancourt was arranging did he explained who Sterling was.

After having won second place in the old time pan around the neck competition, they were finally persuaded to accept Sterling as their arranger.

For a consecutive four years Sterling was to arrange gratuitously for La Creole, sharing with them his time, dedication and love of the pan, they collected many trophies while for Sterling, the need to return to his home land was beginning to be felt.

In Zurich in 1993, he had written lyrics for the song 'More Steel Band Than Snow' that he recorded during one of his voyage to Port of Spain, it was sang by the Calypsonian, Crazy.

He decided that it would be the tune for La Creole to play at the1995 panorama competition. After having all agreed on 'More Steel Band Than Snow' a few members later on decided against it with the excuse that it did not get enough air play on the radio.

Sterling received this with an enormous disenchantment and ended altogether his contribution to arrange for them again.

He often speaks of how people in a way resent the help you may have given in the past. (No good deed goes unpunished).

But through all this. after Derek's death, he was to meet Brian Awang, new PR for La Creole and who became his closest and truest friend, a man of integrity, a pan lover, juggling many skills, as a banker and also at the time, chairman for the tourist board.

It is at Brian's that, for few months every year Sterling stays in Port of Spain, enjoying the preliminaries to the Panorama steel band competitions and the preparation towards carnival.

In November that year The Trinidad and Tobago Folk Art institute in New York invited the seven survivors of TASPO to receive a salute for their contribution as trail blazers for spreading the steel pan art form all over the world;

Andrew de Labastide from Texas

Ellie Manette and Theodore Stevens from the US,

Belgrave Bonaparte and Duddley Smith from the Bahamas who did not attend

Philmore Davidson (Boots) died that same week,

Sterling from England.

A concert and diner were given, Rudy Smith, Robert Greenidge and a steel band from New York gave each an amazing steel band performance, including other acts.

"It was the first time, since I had left TASPO in Paris, that I was reunited with some of the players, I listen to the stories of their journey back to Trinidad from Bordeaux in 1951 and what had finally brought them to move to where they were living now. It was also my first time in New York, I had heard so many different opinions on the city, I was happy to experience the energy that everyone often describes and on which point most agree with."

Sterling was to return three years later in, October 1996, for the Hall of Fame Sunshine Award, presented by the Calypsonian, Horace Liverpool, known as' Chalk Dust'.

In the meantime, in London, he was presented with an Honorary Fellowship from the University of East London, UEL.

Chapter XVIII
Nostalgia

It always had been a struggle to generate sponsorship or enough funds to provide for Nostalgia the necessary equipment and all that was needed for the only 'pan around the neck' band, to come on the road for carnival; even the gigs that Nostalgia performed in were not enough to meet the bands expenses.

Often members had to contribute to the cost of their costumes.

Nostalgia held a very special place in Sterling's heart and financial rewards were never the purpose of his dedication, the reason why his teaching and arranging for the band had never been remunerated. It was primarily that his expectations in the performances of its members were high, always wanting to build his band to another level. However, times had changed and in order to go forward, things also had to change and progress. Sterling's natural inclination and genuine enthusiasm for helping and giving, was challenged by the need for Nostalgia to improve and also for him to be compensated for all his time and efforts, realising that for many, his altruistic aims were not boosting the dedication that he had felt in the past years.

It is well known that freeness is not always compatible with achievement.

"Somehow that year, the number of gigs increased for Nostalgia to perform in and for the first time we managed to raise a more realistic sum.

I also had approached the British Association of Steel Bands, responsible for organizing the London Panorama, in order to get Nostalgia to appear at the competition.

The steel band competition scheduled before carnival represents strictly all the large conventional bands, so when my request for including our pan around the neck band was accepted, I was thrilled.

It also meant appearance fees.

To my great surprise the news were not greeted by some members of the band with the same enthusiasm, they thought that it was far too ambitious of me to put Nostalgia in the same category as the larger conventional bands competing at Panorama, that I was holding high hopes that could only bring disappointment. I did not get disheartened and carried on arranging new tunes, teaching Sandflo in Zurich and Nostalgia in London, my composition 'More Steel Band Than Snow', which brought more recriminations.

More were to come my way when after carnival, I submitted my fees for arranging and teaching, after many excruciating debates I was finally granted my request and shared the remaining sums with the members of the band."

Sterling was busy travelling and did not focus on the band's politics, neither on any of the resentment felt by some members or foreseen the sudden strife for leadership.

Pettiness and jealousy are foreign emotions to Sterling, therefore cannot imagine anyone with such characteristics, the lack of these perceptions has and would work against him over the years.

On his return from Trinidad in 1995 he was to find that some of the Nostalgia players had left, creating their own single pan band.

He was terribly disappointed that his old friend Russel had not maintained himself above all politics and followed the others, after this, their friendship was never to be the same again.

Despite all adversity, with the help of others, Sterling recruited new players and 'Pan Culture', a pan around the neck band from Dortmund, Germany also merged in with Nostalgia for the carnival and would come every summer.

Dortmund was to become Sterling's new destination for teaching and rehearsing new tunes.

"Only during that first carnival with Pan Culture did I realised how much new energy and new talents had been vital to resource Nostalgia's essence and atmosphere, in a way the previous separation had a positive and necessary upshot.

That carnival weekend had been enlivened and I had been deeply moved when back to our hall at Maxilla Social Club in North Kensington, I was given a warm and sincerely cheerful response.

A couple of years later, Pan Culture organised a steel band festival in Dortmund in which they played a variation of classical and modern pieces, Nostalgia was invited, so Andy Narell and his band from Paris.

Lionel McCalman, who I had taught the steel drum and had all along remained with Nostalgia, was at the time a tremendous force behind the band, if not so much as a player as with an indefatigable capacity to deploy his time and energy, between his teaching at University and Nostalgia.

I felt a tremendous confidence in him and he eventually, became an important figure in the band, so important that ten years later he, with the same energy and determination decided that he should become the leader and arranger of the band."

In 2005 Ken Livingston, Mayor of London had the innovative idea to stage a Caribbean festival in Hyde Park over the carnival week end, involving various bands and acts, with stalls selling Caribbean food and souvenirs. An interesting attempt to give families, and people who wished, to take part in the carnival festivities, the opportunity to enjoy the weekend in a more peaceful atmosphere and not having to endure the crowded streets.

After a meeting with the Mayor's office, the members of the BAS (British Association of Steel Band) wanted full control over the funding of this event, in return the Mayor's office demanded to have access to the BAS books, which was declined. The BAS boycotted the festival and whoever had the audacity to perform at this event would definitely be kicked out of the British Association of Steel.

When, Sterling was approached, as a pan pioneer, to open the festival in Hyde Park with Nostalgia, it triggered his interest, always driven to experiment new ventures and to boost the band's stamina with new opportunities and new excitements, he thought this new venue was a great idea. Opposing all ideas that the Hyde Park Festival could result in causing a threat to the Notting Hill Carnival, as many thought it might be, Sterling on the contrary, thought it will enhance its amplitude and that it spreading to the park will therefore contribute to its popularity.

Families who did not like to be squashed in the constricted streets, could peacefully participate to the festivities in the park, enjoying the attractions performing on the huge stage and the food stalls...

Holding a meeting with Nostalgia's members to discuss this topic, Sterling was baffled at the animosity it created amongst the players and the negative response he received from many.

The integrity of the band was shaken by discord, most were afraid of the threat caused by the BAS, others naively believed the rumours that the carnival will be entirely taken away from the streets of Notting Hill. Sterling listened, shaken by the antagonism that his decision had provoked, feeling a threat hanging over his head he then announced that he will be opening the Hyde Park venue on the Monday morning, with the Angels and friends and that whoever wanted to join him was welcome, and, that when finished he would later on that morning meet Nostalgia on the road.

Knowing Sterling well, I knew that nothing would make him change his mind and especially when opposition came in the form of threats.

Lionel threatened not to play Sterling's arrangement on the road.

It had become a power struggle between Sterling and Lionel, a clash of egos, Lionel with the idea that Sterling would bend to his will having succeeded in implanting doubt in most of the weaker members, Sterling galloping away from restraint and control, determined nevertheless to follow his own conviction.

There Lionel saw the opportunity in establishing himself as leader of the band and following some utopian idea that he could also become its arranger.

I do not believe that his misinterpretation of Sterling's reaction could have been so far off the reality, Lionel is an intelligent and perceptive man therefore I believe that he anticipated Sterling's stubbornness, a well-known trait!

Sterling played at the Hyde Park venue with the Angels and friends and later that morning joined a cheerless Nostalgia as they had just left their mass camp off Ladbroke Grove. The reception they were greeted with was certainly not from a dignified adult behaviour and despite the negative ambiance the Angels bravely played the new tune staying closely by Sterling.

This incident ended Nostalgia's blossoming years, the fact that the name could be associated with strife and be soiled, truly pained Sterling, he felt betrayed by the very one he taught music to and trusted, it took great strength to overcome the loss.

Over the years I have witnessed how painful it had been for Sterling to accept. When I had asked him if he would eventually get back with Nostalgia, he shook his head and uttered his famous NO.NO.NO.

"After seeing the bad spirit that had overcome the players I could not for one instant be part of the band without betraying my own integrity, all I saw were disputes and separation. The years of teaching and carrying a band were over for me."

When Sterling wanted to take the name back he was to find out that a company had been formed registering the band's name at the same time.

"The only thing I wanted was to take the name away for it not to be soiled.

Philmore/Boots, who had christened our band was no longer with us in 2005 to witness how Nostalgia had lost its momentum.

When in London I have become a spectator at carnival, my friend Brian also joins me in London every August. There is no more room for a pan around the neck band as the DJs and steel bands trucks overpower everything, sometimes I find it difficult to remember how it was years ago and how little did we know, Russel and I, that the little children carnival we played for in 1963 will become the biggest festival in Europe…"

Chapter XIX
Elisa and the Angels

"I met Elisabeth Pfafflin, the German psycho-dramatist while playing with Sandflo in Niederdorf, the old district of Zurich; it was at the 1988 February carnival.

Her approach was with the straightforwardness that characterises her and with which, over the years I became familiar with:

"I can see that you are the one carrying this band so the ONE I need to talk to," she said, spoken without any other introduction in her very approximate English, explaining her total bemusement at the sound of the steel band, never having heard or seen one before. She spoke of a xylophone that her friend, André Thomkins the surrealist painter, had built and that it reminded her of a similar sound.

I told her that she could also play, while negatively shaking her head, she confessed that she was aware of not having any sense of rhythm or any musical inclination whatsoever, it was something that she would not even contemplate.

It was the introduction to a long and true friendship and her introduction to music.

In London, for her, I ordered a second pan from the pan maker and tuner, Bertrand Parris, who had made drums for Sandflo and for other bands in Switzerland.

I gave Elisa her first lesson.

Teaching Elisa was quite challenging, as she had warned me, she had no sense of rhythm or timing, the two essential elements required in music and at some point in the middle of rehearsals she would, out of sheer frustration and despair, burst into tears. Her usual determination and persistence brought her to play the following year with Nostalgia for her first Notting Hill Carnival in 1989."

Every weekend Elisabeth retreats to her farmhouse near Constance, a refuge of tranquillity for many of her colleagues and friends passing through, relishing the peaceful and natural environment that surrounds Elizabeth's house and her savoury cooking. There, one can immerse himself in a time long forgotten to city gremlins; there are baskets of wood to bring in from the massive heap of logs stacked neatly in the barn adjacent to the house, to feed the beautifully decorated ceramic blue and white stove that heats the whole house; baskets full of apples, pears and mushrooms that someone had just collected, or strawberries and all summer fruits that Eliza will make her tasty jam with.

There is the ever so rich pantry with homemade everything, the cellars with vegetables and wine, the on-going activities around the kitchen table as children from nearby farms walked in when it suits them eating the cakes that Elisa had baked that morning and meeting people from different part of the world, listening to the different languages spoken around them.

Night or day the front door is never locked.

You sleep with the moon playing through the slants in the shutters and wake up with the cowbells from the fields.

I have understood how Elisabeth had recreated a childhood dream.

"One afternoon while I was giving Elisabeth a lesson in the music room, two little girls walked in, Karin eight years old and her sister Doris, slightly younger, they just stood shyly at the top of the stairs looking at us listening with great interest. I played some tunes for them, urged them to come forward and look at the pans, when I saw the interest and eagerness at which they were scrutinising my every movement and how absorbed they were, I lowered the stand on which the drums were placed and gave them the sticks to try for themselves.

They returned the next day to head straight to the music room, seeing their enthusiasm, Elisabeth decided to have some drums made for them.

Of course Karin and Doris brought other children from the hamlet, it became the talk of the neighbourhood farms, some parents were reticent in letting their children near me, never having known or seen a black man before.

They had gradually got accustom to see colourful people coming and going from Elisabeth house but never yet black people and little did they know that in time they would encounter and be friended with many."

Oetlishausen is a hamlet of three farms including Elisa's.

From her dining room windows you can see rising above her garden a little church encircled by well-kept flowers and greenery, a little further behind high trees the still vacant large house with, despite the abandoned and overgrown grounds, an intact kitchen garden where Elisa would pick her herbs for cooking.

The surrounding landscape is of rolling hills and green pastures where cows graze carrying huge bells around their necks, fields of apple, pear and plum plantations only separated by the dark and compact woodland, neatly shaped in a rectangle stretching for a few acres or forming a complete forest.

In the background looms the 2505 meters tall mountain of the Santis, the Appenzell Alps and from its top one can see all the Alps and also Austria and Germany.

The nearest village is a quarter of a mile away, where cheeses are made and purchased directly from the owner and fresh milk in a tin container, Elisabeth gets her meat, fruits and vegetables from the nearby farms and it is a ritual to assist her carrying two huge baskets going from one farm for eggs to another one for tomatoes and so on...(with the help of her car)!

"Few months after my first visit to Oetlishausen, I got acquainted with some other children, mostly between six and eight years old, who had decided to learn to play the steel drum with the ambition to form a little group, I was there to encourage them, so was Elisabeth. They learned fast, some were also learning piano, the recorder, or the guitar, which helped.

Elisa dedicated one of her huge rooms for my workshop, storing the large number of drums we had acquired, she also introduced many of her friends to the steel drum, amongst them I taught a couple from Amsterdam who ordered their own drums, I was to befriend them and on few occasions visited them on their houseboat bringing with me Junior Gill or Russel, or the little group from Oetlishausen who had named themselves 'The Jolly Jumpers'.

Junior and I gigged in Amsterdam too.

Elisabeth's love story with Andre Thomkins, the painter had ended tragically a few years before I met her, there are pictures of him stuck on the kitchen wall over the table, she often mentioned his name and his paintings adorned the wooden walls of her study.

The Andre Thomkins exhibition she was to organise with the Berlin Academy of Arts, finally materialised and I, playing for its opening brought two of my steel band friends. In addition to the artist's paintings, the xylophone he had constructed was also exhibited on which we played, improvising.

(When in 2013, the Liechtenstein Kunstmuseum in Vaduz purchased that same xylophone, I was asked to attend the June inauguration to play the instrument, I invited two friends, the talented steel drum players, Junior Gill and Tamla Batra).

At the same time the Berlin wall was coming down and having left my drum in the hotel I felt frustrated for not taking part and sharing with music the exhilaration of the moment, it was an incredible event and I just stood there defeated not to have followed my first impulse. It was 1989.

Also in Oetlishausen, I celebrated my memorable 60s birthday.

Elisabeth who loves a party organised it, inviting some of my friends from London and from Nostalgia, Beatrice,

Katherine, Benjamin and his girlfriend, Olivia, (his leg in a cast from a motorbike accident) came too, players from Zurich and many of Elisa's friends.

In spite of the fact that the house is by no means small, to accommodate more people Elisabeth turned her attic into a dormitory, the many others were housed in the nearest town and by the farmers who by then had become less reticent towards 'the foreigners'.

They generously opened their extremely clean and tidy houses to all, some few kilometres away, which brought a bit of confusion when, in the early hours of the morning, people had to find their way under the moon and the influence of too many Schnapps!

The rented village hall had been decorated, food and drinks catered for, Nostalgia, Sandflo, The Jolly Jumpers and a jazz band from Germany all played that evening and the next day in Elisabeth's barn, as the party extended throughout the weekend.

Elisabeth gave many other parties after that…

After ten years of playing steel band, The Jolly Jumpers youth group, had acquired a huge repertoire and with maturity their talent had flourished adding to the advantage of having, from an early age, played other instruments.

In 1999, three of my pupils left, Karin, my first pupil had become the leader of the band, Ramon, Sabrina, Janine and Doris remained and they all decided that the name Jolly Jumpers was far too childish and renamed the band Sterling's Angels. Youngest sister Ramona joined the group also.

It was on one of these afternoon that between rehearsals in Oetlishausen we all sat for a break around the kitchen table, drinking tea and eating the delicious homemade cakes that after bombarding names at each other, Ramona came up with the title, Sterling's Girls, it was greeted with roaring laughter from the elders to a bewildered Ramona, I had to pass on that.

A week later in Bern, meeting Darkie, an excellent pan tuner from Trinidad, chatting while he was tuning some pans, I told him how the girls were in search of a new title for their band, making him laugh at Ramona's suggestion. "What about Sterling's Angels?" said he.

When I told the Angels about Darkie's idea, without hesitation they all agreed on it.

Karin had to wait until her 16th birthday to be allowed to travel to London and play at the Notting Hill Carnival, despite the fact that she would stay with us, her parents still needed a lot of convincing to let her go and with the reassurance that Beatrice and Elisa would be watching her every steps, she was able to travel.

It was to be Karin's first time to leave home let alone fly to another country, the very first time for her parents and sisters to leave Switzerland for a joint London birthday party with Katherine's 50th and my 70th in 1990.

Growing up, the Angels were eventually allowed to come to London to take part in the Notting Hill Carnival and faithfully every year until 2005, the Angels joined Nostalgia and all stayed with us at Mortimer Road.

Even Karin's teenage sister, Ramona, came.

For his thesis, Ramon chose the history of pan and received a great appraisal for a well-executed work, he gave me a copy which I thought was written with evident passion.

Later on, Doris also choose the same subject for her thesis and both were received with honours.

Between school and university the Angels were ferociously gigging, following the first few assignments, to carry their drums they bought a trailer with a white canopy with, Sterling's Angels Steel Band, written in black.

Karin visited Trinidad and Tobago while I was there in 2003, played with La Creole Pan Grove, experienced J'ouvert morning, the carnival and the beautiful beaches of both islands.

At every opportunity she travels to South America, practises Tango, and speaks fluent Spanish, French and English.

Finishing her law studies and working for a law firm for a couple of years, she now is back studying for a PHD.

Sabrina is also fluent in three languages and is a doctor in Bern,

Janine is a speech therapist

Doris teaches young children.

Ramona is in hotel management.

In spite of their busy schedules and their different locations, when Sterling is visiting Oetlishausen they will drop any other obligations for a musical reunion at Elisabeth's and as Karin said "Exploring another dimension and once again feel in tune with the universe immersing oneself into another world," she had cherished for many years and still does.

In 2004 they released a CD 'Live Nice', they only wanted the pure sound of the pan without any electrical instruments, for which I arranged the tunes and played the Congo drums".

Chapter XX
Le Petit Dauphin

For three months every winter, Sterling escapes the British weather and visits Trinidad staying in Diego Martin at his friend Brian's.

Diego Martin, a town, north-west of Port of Spain, is built in a valley in the Northern Range, an area of tall forested hills, stretching from the Chaguaramas peninsula to Toco in the west, to Arima in the east where, in this valley is nestled the Asa Wright Nature Centre one of the premier bird watching spots in the Caribbean.

The two peaks of El Cerro del Aripo and El Tucuche rise up to 940 meters, the later also known by the Amerindian name of 'humming bird', was then considered a sacred mountain and the home of the Golden Frog.

The youngest of seven brothers and sisters, Brian left Trinidad at eighteen to study economics in Ottawa Canada.

After having graduated in Chartered Accountancy he came back to the island to stay and pursued a career in accountancy and banking.

I had met Brian on one of my short visits to Trinidad before seeing him again on his various trips to London and understood how, it was primarily their mutual passion for steel band and music in general that had brought him and Sterling together and at how they interact so well on the subject.

An example at how one common interest can often be enough to unite unlikely people, becoming in this case, the base of the relationship and despite all divergences will sustain it throughout the years.

It was to be through music with 'La Creole Pan Grove' that Brian and Sterling became acquainted. When Sterling's close friend, Derek Medina died, Brian replaced him as PR for the band and at the same time joined the group as a bass pan player.

Despite the years of studying in Canada and the demands of work, Brian had continuously kept a defined and privileged space for his natural inclination to music.

His suppressed creativity also explodes with his love for cooking, totally immersing himself in meticulously prepared dishes done so with such a concentration and involvement that his pleasure is undeniable.

I have not yet seen a cooking program surpassing his art form at dicing vegetables so minutely equal, displaying all in dishes in a harmony of colour and with succulent results!

"I met Brian nine years ago and for the last five years stayed in his house in Diego Martin, despite his busy work schedule as CEO at the Exim Bank of Port of Spain and chairman of the tourist board, he is very involved with steel band and has entered many competitions with his band, La Creole.

I do not know how he does it all but Brian is constantly active, his nights are short getting up at 4 am, subsequently, during the day or evening he will fall asleep anywhere...maybe an escape from certain moments, from people or when boredom sets in!

His mother told me that he did it when he was a child.

In the summer he visits London and shares some time with Beatrice and I in France, the attraction to the French supermarket and the quaint little shops in the small town, where everyone now knows him, have become his target and his downfall, as extra suitcases are often needed, to accommodate all his purchases on his return home!

Usually overloaded, on the Eurostar back to London, with anything that would have taken Brian's fancy, from food to natural essence, linens, candles, objects; I watched the regret with which once, he had to let go of an armchair in the antique shop and had to pull him away.

Clearly his inclination towards the good and beautiful things of the world often lead him to many irresistible temptations.

When I accompany him to the St Juan market in Port of Spain early on Sunday morning, I cannot stop Brian's compulsive shopping as he always will have a good excuse to oppose my reservation!

Brian has also the ability to be very convincing!"

Recently while alone in the house in Diego Martin, Sterling had a stroke and when Brian, on his return home from Brazil, found him in a state of utter confusion, without hesitation and despite Sterling's reticence, organised that same day, scans and every possible tests; services that are not readily obtainable at such short notice in Port of Spain.

Sterling needed major surgery within the next three days, as blood was slowly invading the left side of his brain and that such operation would be best performed in London despite the risk of taking him on a nine hour flight.

There was no hesitation or time for Brian to speculate and with the X rays and scan's results under his arm, boarded the next flight to London hiding the fact that Sterling had lost his usual clear faculties and stability, for fear of being prevented to fly, "People just thought he was drunk or incapacitated," explained Brian.

Sterling has no recollection of that flight, not even when Brian had to feed him, keeping a tight vigil all through the night until his arrival at Gatwick Airport.

"Le petit dauphin est malade." Brian kept quoting this phrase that had remained in his mind from his high school French classes.

For Brian, life is a permanent victory, downfalls have not altered his love of the world and of all things.

Two months later after his operation and before participating in the Jools Holland BBC TV documentary *London Calling,* Sterling had previously contributed in the BBC 2 program *1951 Festival of Britain: A Brave New World* and during the interview sang his new calypso song on TASPO Story which was eventually launched on the 26th March 2013 at the Trinidad and Tobago High Commission.

TASPO STORY

Long ago steel band
Had a bad reputation
If you dare beat a pan
You were labelled a vagabond
Humiliation never ceased
Licks from wicked police
Steel bands had horrors
Now we salute our pan pioneers

Now Anthony Williams
Had a very special gift
He made oversized drum
Tuned and called it the fourths and fifths
He also was the first to make a pair of cello pans
He was a genius experimenting with the steel band

One we can't forget, his name is Ellie Mannette
Is an important man
In the evolution of pan
They started on small paint pans
Ellie and Francis Wickham
They were the first to tie rubber on a stick
To beat pan

Many people who, had contributed a lot
They talk with the pan men
So they could stop the riots
The honourable Albert Gomes
The brainchild of TASPO
Steel band president Sydney Gollop
He had told us so

The name was
Trinidad all steel percussion orchestra (TASPO)
That is the name we always remember
Trinidad all steel percussion orchestra (TASPO)
That is the name that will live on forever and ever
This anniversary
Will go down in history
This sixty anniversary will stay in our memory
Trinbago steel band (yes it is) our greatest musical
Invention in we island

Sixty years ago
I want the whole world to know
In 1951 for the Festival of Britain
The steel band association
Said a steel band must go
After many suggestions
They named a steel band Taspo

Then twelve pan men were chosen
From many different steel bands
Those who weren't selected
Weren't in the association

Granville Sealey from Tripoli
Ask for plenty money (stupide)
They dropped him from Taspo
And boy, that was the end of he

Lieutenant Griffith
Was musical director
He was from Barbados
But they brought him from St Lucia
The man was a great musician
And taught them very quick
He said for the festival
They'll have to play good music

When the steel band left
Was on the sixth of July
Big crowd came on the docks
Emotion, women started to cry
TASPO had some rusty steel drums
Was a clever gimmick
Spectators in London said
Was witchcraft and black magic (but it was)

Trinidad All Steel Percussion Orchestra (Taspo)
That is the name we will always remember
Trinidad All Steel Percussion Orchestra (TASPO)
That is the name that will live on forever and never
This anniversary
Will go down in history
This sixty anniversary will stay in our memory
Trinbago steel band (yes it is) our great musical

Invention in we island

This very funny
A joke I must share with you
In the Lyceum ballroom
What I am telling you is true
First time to calypso
Could not whine or jump up
An Englishman snatched his wife
And start to dance the foxtrot

Something you didn't know
About the steel band Taspo
They got an engagement
For a very important show
The band was very excited
Was sixty years ago
They played in Paris
At a circus named the Medrano

Five wanted to stay
But after when they were told
By the Lord Kichener
Dededede bad john in England is the cold (they shiver)
That made their minds to go back home
And improve their band
But one man stayed on to introduce
Steel band in Britain

Music and lyrics

Are by Sterling Betancourt
On behalf of TASPO
We thank the people of Trinbago
They knew they had something special
Now their story unfold (by me Crazy)
TASPO the trailblazer have steel band
All over the world (don't doubt it)

Chorus

MORE STEEL BAND THAN SNOW

I told my friends but they laugh and they say am crazy
That steel band spreading all over Switzerland
It didn't start so long ago
But it have more steel band there now than it have snow
The steel band spread through the land like a great fire
You'll be shocked the amount of band they got there
Now this is a fact what I am telling you
It started with Sterling Betancourt

    Chorus

  You leave the Banhof
  And you walk through Niederdorf
  When you reach Cantina sweet music in the air
  You go to Rapperswill
  And you drive up to Basel
  Wherever you go
  More steel band than snow

I'll tell you now exactly when it really start
In Zurich 76 hotel Nova Park
Sterling went to play with a steel band
When a Swiss ask he to make him a tenor pan

With steel drum and hammer by the road he started to
pound
Every now and then some people came around
Some shouted "Gruetzi" as they were passing by
And some of them rang for Swiss Polizei

The policemen went up to him in cool manner
One hand on his gun: "What are you doing there?"
But in Switzerland you must always walk with your
working
Permit documents and passport
He told the police he was making instrument
So he checked his paper and then he went
But before he go he had a smile on his face
He said: "I thought you were opening a money safe."

The first steel band in Zurich was Tropical Fever
It chanced to Sandflo and Bollito Misto
The hot bananas, yes they also split up
And those who left they call themselves Coconut and
Crazy Bees
Evolution, Pan Network and Pina Colada
You should hear them jamming last November
For it is tradition, eleven past eleven O'clock
On the eleven of November
All the bands get together and play.

Chorus

Lots of steel bands in Lucern
Steel pan factory down in Bern

Pan shops everywhere
Well its steel band mania
If you go to ski
You better take this advice from me
Wherever you go
PURE STEEL BANDS! NO SNOW!

SANKEE SOCA

I was lying in bed and I couldn't sleep a wink
I was tossing and turning and then I start to think
In a church not too far the bell began to chime
And these Sankee Socas came to my mind
I can remember still at the foot of Laventille
Baptists stand there singing their Sankee song
All the members they dressed in white
On the ground candle burning bright
As they clap and sing to their Sankee Soca song
All the members they dressed in white
Oh! What a lovely sight
As they clap and sing their Sankee Soca song

Chorus
It was come and dine, come and dine
We will feast at Jesus table all the time
As he fed the multitude turning water into wine
All you hungry souls, come and dine.

That was the Sankee Soca, beautiful Sankee Soca
Wonderful Sankee Soca behind the dry river
They sang the Sankee Soca, glorious Sankee Soca
Spiritual Sankee Soca, behind the dry river.

And they would pray, and their bell would ring
And then they would chant and clap and then they
Would start to sing
And then they would pray, for a Holy day
We must thank Panday for giving the Baptists a holiday

I would just love to see, now those days come back again
When they preached peace and love, on the streets of
Port of Spain.
And I'm sure you'll agree, there's no better therapy,
To get people to live in harmony
All the killings would stop, and the crime rate would
drop
And we'll walk in the night without a fright.

I don't know who we must blame, all I know that it is a
shame
For not hearing more of these Sankee Soca songs
I don't know now who we must blame, all I know that it
is a shame
For not hearing more of these Sankee Soca songs

Chorus
It was come and dine, come and dine
We will feast at Jesus table all the time
As he fed the multitude, turning water into wine
All you hungry souls, come and dine.

They were praying for years, but no one answered their
prayers
Persecution was great but they never ever lose faith